The Holy Catechism
of Yeshua Barnasha

To my mother,
who taught me to seek the Spirit in all things,
and to my father,
who taught me to test all things.

The Holy Catechism of Yeshua Barnasha

Clayton Todd Kirk

LUCAS
PARK
BOOKS
ST. LOUIS, MISSOURI

ISBN: 978-1-60350-010-4

Published by Lucas Park Books
www.lucasparkbooks.com

Contents

Acknowledgements

Above all, a heartfelt thanks to my wonderful wife September Lynne who graciously helped with proof-reading and copy-editing, as well as enduring countless hours of listening to my re-reads and ideas. I am forever in your debt.

A special thanks to Dr. Jonathan Wade, David Dean, and Kent Kirk for valuable feedback and constructive intellectual banter. Their honesty and helpful reflections took the present project from mere "interesting idea" to its present completed form.

Thanks also to the late Fr. Ralph Dodd who challenged my faith regularly. Fr. Ralph had the honesty to answer tough questions and the guts to demand answers of his own.

Thank you to all the brave intellectual giants that inspired me in my youth and beyond. I've never met you in person, but you are brothers to me through your works. Thank you, C.S. Lewis, Jim Marion, Swami Vivekananda, Thornton Wilder, Carl Sagan, Kenneth Ring, Melvin Morse, Itzhak Bentov, Thomas Keating, Donald Miller, Richard Alpert, Marcus Borg, and M. Night Shyamalan.

Thank you to Yeshua Barnasha, who gave his life for what is True.

Foreword

The book you hold in your hand is an honest and careful attempt to reconstruct the actual words of Jesus divorced from the accretions of history and the weight of theological motivations. All projects and formulations begin with assumptions and the present work is no exception. As assumptions are often partially subconscious and difficult to identify, the author wishes to bring his to the light at the outset.

First, it is the position of the author that Jesus' original message was corrupted fairly early in the development of Christianity; particularly the period of approximately 30 to 100 A.C.E. **Second,** it is the belief of the author that Jesus' teaching shows essential consensus with mystics of both the Eastern and Western traditions both ancient and modern. **Third,** the author holds that it is possible, at least to some extent, to recapture the essence of Jesus' original message using rational, systematic processes.

Many Christians, particularly in the U.S.A., will, in all likelihood, disagree with some or all of the abovementioned assumptions. However, these positions are not rare in the scholarly community or in many worshipping communities of the so-called "New Age" or Progressive Christians. In addition, these assumptions are not at all new. Most were already being batted around among the scholars as far back as the 1700's A.C.E. The author feels convicted that as our new century slowly begins to assert its personality, the consensus of persons who share some or all of these assumptions will continue to build momentum.

The book is divided into five chapters and an afterword. The core of the book is Chapter Three, which presents the words and life of the historical Jesus in a reconstructed chronological order. Chapter One provides a prologue with an overall rationale for the project. Chapter Two provides detailed information about how the words of Jesus were decided upon and arranged.

As mentioned previously, Chapter Three provides a readable story of the life of Jesus in chronological order. Chapter Four provides a helpful and accessible topical organization of the key themes in the teachings of the historical Jesus. Chapter Five presents Jesus' key ideas in a traditional Christian catechismal (learning guide) format. The project concludes with an afterword of the author's reflections on who the real Jesus was, and how he differs from the Christ-of-Faith. Although some might have preferred that the book begin with the material in the *Afterword,* the author did not want to risk leading the reader into any particular conclusions about who Jesus was until they had had a fair chance to meet him on their own.

I commend to you this three-year labor of love. May it enrich your spiritual walk, bring you peace, and fortify your search.

Clayton Todd Kirk
January 8, 2010

1

Prologue to a True Story

Five year olds ask questions the rest of us have forgotten. They feel no connection to the political climate. Nor have they been on Earth long enough to know what they *should* ask. They have not yet been taught to feel guilty about asking the wrong questions. They are pure. They see things as they are. Jesus recognized this in children.

I began this project as a legacy to my children. As I finished different parts of it, I would read excerpts from the words of Jesus aloud at the dinner table. Although my original goal was to accurately and honestly guide my children's moral development, I found that after a time it was they that were guiding me.

I discovered over time that unlike my curious and innocent children, many adults, myself included, seem to spend our time on Earth in a series of delusions of varying intensity and duration. We negotiate and compromise with society in our subconscious. We re-learn who we are in piecemeal, and that very slowly. This is, in fact, one of the great teachings of the world's major religions: Life is a journey of spiritual evolution and self-discovery (or perhaps, re-discovery). This assertion takes different forms and is

1

sometimes covered by tangential doctrines, but remains at the core of Faith.

I have become convinced that Jesus' core message was one of spiritual evolution, learning, and personal responsibility. Jesus himself went through a period of facing his own doubts and purpose which culminated in the "Temptation in the Desert," recorded in the Fourth chapter of the book of Matthew. He practiced what he preached. He lived what he taught.

However, on a global scale, there are marked differences in the *interpretations* of who Jesus actually was and what he taught. One might say that there are several different "Jesuses," each defined by different theologies, doctrines, and emphases. In our present time, these diverse Jesuses can be condensed (for the purpose of argument) into two broad categories: 1) The Jesus of compassion and non-judgment, and 2) the Jesus of atonement and reprobation.

This second "Jesus;" the Jesus of atonement and reprobation, is probably the most familiar to many Christians. The basic "Atonement Creed" is similar to the doctrinal statements of many major Christian organizations, and can be summed as follows:

> Jesus, who was uniquely divine, died for our sins to appease the anger (i.e. sense of justice) of his father, the only god of the universe. If we accept Jesus and his faith (i.e., system of salvation) we will be saved. If we do not, or can not, we will not be saved (i.e. from Hell). There is no other way to be saved except through this substitutionary sacrifice.[1]

Many Christians would also add the following corollary:

> We are totally depraved as humans and completely incapable of approaching God on our own merits. Salvation is therefore a free gift that cannot be earned. It can in no way be merited by our personal behavior.[2]

But, from where does this widespread and widely promulgated version of Jesus' teaching originate and how is it related to the aforementioned Jesus of compassion and tolerance?

Almost everything known about Jesus' sayings comes from Matthew, Mark, Luke, and John in the Christian "New Testament." The first three books, Matthew, Mark, and Luke, are generally thought to be older (and therefore more historically accurate) than John; Mark being the oldest by 15 to 20 years.[3] These three oldest gospels, taken together, are known as the "synoptic" gospels. **None of the assumptions in the abovementioned "Atonement Theology" creeds can be clearly defended with information from Matthew, Mark and Luke.** And even in the book of John, with its more developed Christology, the theology of atonement is much less clear and specific than is warranted by the Atonement Creed. This is the Great Enigma that precipitated the writing of this book.

Most of the information in the Atonement Creed comes not from Jesus, but from the interpretations of Jesus' message in the writings of Paul (and those directly influenced by Paul.)[4] Therefore many, if not all, of the core assumptions of the Faith held by a majority of Christians worldwide have almost no basis in the teachings of the man Jesus as recorded in the three synoptic gospels (Matthew, Mark, and Luke).

In fact, if all we had as source materials for the theology of Jesus were the three oldest and most reliable books; Matthew, Mark, and Luke, then many of the core doctrines of traditional Christianity would evaporate. The following two examples are submitted as preliminary evidence of this contention:

Subsitutionary Sacrifice

No doctrine is stressed more in modern Christianity than the substitutionary sacrifice of Jesus.[5] However it has scarce support in the three synoptic gospels. In fact in many instances Jesus tells people that *they* are responsible for their *own* salvation. Here are some supporting quotes from the words of Jesus as recorded in the synoptics:

Matthew 12:37, *For by thy words thou shalt be justified, and by thy words thou shalt be condemned* (ASV).

Matthew 16:27, *For the Son of man shall come in the glory of his Father with his angels; and then shall he render unto every man according to his deeds* (ASV).

Unique Divinity

Jesus is generally thought by Christians to be uniquely divine and thus uniquely worthy of worship and supplication. However, when Jesus himself was reported as being worshipped in the book of Luke, he corrects the would-be worshipper and directs them again to monitor their *own* behavior:

Luke 11:27-28, *And it came to pass, as he said these things, a certain woman out of the multitude lifted up her voice, and said unto him, "Blessed is the womb that bare thee, and the breasts which thou didst suck". But he said, "Yea rather, blessed are they that hear the word of God, and keep it"* (ASV).

In addition, the title Jesus used for himself frequently was not the title "Son of God," but rather the humbling term, "a son of man," or "Barnasha" in his native language of Aramaic.[6] According to many scholars this term is best translated as "human," or perhaps even "mere human," or "mortal:"

Matthew 8:20, *The foxes have holes and the birds of the air have nests, but the Son of man hath nowhere to lay his head* (KJV).

On the other hand, on almost every page of the synoptic gospels, Jesus teaches cause-and-effect, correct intentions, and personal responsibility. Taken together, this combination of values is very similar to the concept of Karma as it is known in many Eastern religions[7]. It is much more similar to the Jesus of Compassion than the Jesus described by the Atonement Creed. Consider the following examples:

Mark 4:24-25, *And he said unto them, Take heed what ye hear: with what measure ye mete, it shall be measured to you: and unto you that hear shall more be given. For he that hath, to him shall be given: and he that hath not, from him shall be taken even that which he hath* (KJV).

Matthew 12:36-37, *But I say unto you that every idle word that men shall speak, they shall give account thereof in the Day of Judgment. For by thy words thou shalt be justified, and by thy words thou shalt be condemned* (KJV).

Matthew 9:11-13, *And when the Pharisees saw it, they said unto His disciples, "Why eateth your master with publicans and sinners?" But when Jesus heard that, He said unto them, "They that be whole need not a physician, but they that are sick. But go ye and learn what this meaneth: `I will have mercy and not sacrifice.' For I am not come to call the righteous, but sinners to repentance"* (KJV).

Mark 7:15-16, *There is nothing from outside a man that, entering into him, can defile him; but the things which come out of him, those are they that defile the man. If any man have ears to hear, let him hear* (KJV).

2

Introduction to Jesus

In his lifetime, the man Christians know as Jesus was most probably called "Yeshua" in his native tongue of Aramaic. Yeshua was a fairly common name and transliterates both into "Jesus" and "Joshua" in English. One of Jesus' most common descriptors of himself was "Son of Man," which is difficult to translate into literal English. The Aramaic word would most likely have been "Barnasha," and may have well have meant something like "mortal man."[1] I had yearned for a learning guide or Catechism from the historical Jesus. In the end, I made my own, using reasonable, almost scientific principles. As I hope the reader will discover, Jesus' actual words are unique and life changing. They deserve to be set apart from the mundane: They are, in fact, *holy*. This is the genesis for the title of the present work: <u>The Holy Catechism of Yeshua Barnasha.</u>

The overriding purpose of this book is the following: To come as close as possible to the spirit of what Jesus actually said, and to build a useable Catechism[2] from the conclusions. In short, to recapture the actual religion of Jesus of Nazareth divorced from the accretions of history, and based upon what he actually said and meant. This task has been undertaken with intense meditation and prayer as well as great trepidation. In the final analysis, it was only undertaken because no other materials of this type were readily available. It is hoped that the reader will accept this project in the spirit in which it was intended: to deepen the devotional life and spiritual evolution of those, who, like the author, are disillusioned with the conflicting messages of the bible and organized religion as well as the inconsistent values promulgated (or at least widely perceived as such) by the same.

It was deemed necessary to first build the most accurate and orderly compilation of what Jesus actually said. In short, an accurate and trustworthy source document was necessary to begin the project. Several authors and scholars have taken on parts of this task. The bibliography provides a summary of the major works in this field, all of which were carefully read, studied and compared by the present author. Among these, two in particular became the guiding documents for this project (with close reference and comparison to the other documents mentioned in the bibliography): The Gospel of Jesus (Funk, 1999) and A Life of Jesus (Goodspeed, 1956). These became valuable sources of information, although neither was quoted from directly. Both of these books represent a conservative assessment, in the judgment of scholars, as to what Jesus actually said. The Gospel of Jesus is particularly useful towards this end in that it represents the conclusions of 150 researchers dedicated to re-discovering what Jesus said divorced from later accretions of history and prior to the onslaught of Pauline theology.[3] Edgar Goodspeed, author of A Life of Jesus, is one of the greatest American biblical scholars of the 20th century, and the first translator of the entire bible into colloquial English.

By comparison with these and other sources, the present author arrived at a conservative consensus of Jesus' sayings to be rendered in modern English. Most of these sayings come from the book of Mark, but a few are derived from the other Gospels as well as a few extra-biblical ancient sources such as The Gospel of Thomas and the Oxyrhynchus fragments[4].

There are three versions of the sayings included in the present work. The first is rendered in a reconstructed chronological order drawing heavily upon a consensus of the chronologies suggested by Goodspeed (1956), Aland (1993), Funk (1999), Wilson (1984), and others (see bibliography for complete list). The second is presented in thematic order, beginning with Jesus' most frequently articulated themes and ending with those less frequently cited. The third is rendered in a traditional Christian catechismal scheme.

To construct the thematic catechism, a list of themes (or topics) were decided upon using a modified "factor analysis." By carefully studying conclusions and suggestions by various noted scholars and thinkers in the field (*cf* Borg (1984), Marion (2004), Wilson (1984), Yogananda (2007), et.al.) regarding the substantive themes of Jesus' teaching, a preliminary list of six possible themes was constructed. Included in this suggested preliminary list were the following themes: **Karma** (defined previously), **God's Nature** (Jesus' unique teachings about what God is like), **The Kingdom of God**, **Non-attachment**, **Compassion**, and **Human Nature** (Jesus' unique teachings about the place and status of humankind).

The constructed document of Jesus' sayings was analyzed by searching for the abovementioned themes and counting the number of pericopes (*i.e.* self contained stories or sayings) deemed to relate to each. The original list turned out to have been a fairly accurate description of Jesus' major themes and topics. However, the analysis generated useful information about the relative frequency-of-occurrence of each. The themes, in order of how often they were articulated by Jesus, are as follows: **1) Karma** (20 pericopes); **2) Kingdom of God** (20 pericopes); **3) God's Nature** (17 pericopes); **4) Human Nature** (14 pericopes); **5) Compassion** (7 pericopes); and, **6) Non-attachment** (4 pericopes). Many of the pericopes related to more than one theme and thus were counted twice.

Salvation

What does it all mean? If Jesus were here (in the flesh) and the question could be put to him: "How is one saved?," or "How does a person achieve contentment?," What would he say, based upon the conclusions of the present project? Fortunately neither blind speculation nor naïve reliance on Church authority is necessary as we have been left everything we need to answer the question intelligently. Hopefully the materials offered in this work will assist the readers in answering the question for themselves. Offered below is the author's reflection on how Jesus might answer the question in modern English idiom, based entirely upon scripture:

> Above all else, dedicate yourself to an honest pursuit of God. Make everyday about finding the Truth. If you have trouble seeing God, then look into the eyes of the people around you. God is there, and so are you. Start by serving others, and your ability to see God will strengthen. It is a gradual process. Love your neighbor as much as you love yourself. The more you loose yourself in this search, the closer to God and the more content you will be. Selfish actions strengthen your carnal self. Selfless actions strengthen your spiritual self which is the only real self anyway. Of all the things to be desired on Earth, only love lasts[5].

3

The Story in
Chronological Order

Following is a reconstruction of the life and sayings of the Historical Jesus in rough chronological order. In the interest of accuracy and scientific conservatism, the author has resisted the natural human urge to "fill in the gaps" in places where the evidence was wanting. This results in a narrative that can be rather choppy in parts. However, it seemed wiser to let the reader speculate for him or herself rather than to risk leading them into error with the best of intentions. Above each pericope the reader will find scriptural cross-references for further investigation. Following this chronological narrative are the essential sayings of the Historical Jesus in topical order.

In the beginning was the Word, and the Word was with God,
and the Word was God.
In him was life; and the life was the light of men.
And the light shineth in darkness;
and the darkness comprehended it not.
He came unto his own, and his own received him not.
But as many as received him,
to them gave he power to become the sons of God,
even to them that believe on his name:
Which were born, not of blood, nor of the will of the flesh,
nor of the will of man, but of God.
And the Word was made flesh, and dwelt among us,
and we beheld his glory,
the glory as of the only begotten of the Father,
full of grace and truth.[1]

Introduction[2]

Matthew 2:23; Luke 1:26; 2:4, 34, 46-52; Galatians 2:7-9

This is the true story of Jesus of Nazareth. It is said that Jesus was closer to God than any one who has ever lived. In fact, Jesus himself claimed to be equal with God. This is the story of his life and what he told his friends about God.

In his time, Jesus was known as "Yeshua." Yeshua was a common name in the Middle East and is the same name as "Joshua" in the English tongue. To the ears of the Greek followers of Yeshua, his name sounded like "Jesus," so when they first wrote it down they spelled it J-E-S-U-S. These are the people who wrote our scriptures and were thus the keepers and protectors of our Faith. Jesus frequently referred to himself as the "Son of Man," or "Barnasha" in his native language.

Jesus was born into a working class family in northern Israel in 6 B.C., a little over 2000 years ago. He grew up in the town of Nazareth and made his living as a carpenter until he was 31 years old. Even as a child, he was known for his wisdom, insatiable curiosity, and compassion for others. Jesus had four brothers and at least two sisters. His brother's names were James, Jude, Simon, and Joses. He was closest to his brother James who would eventually be the first person to organize a congregation in the name of his earthly and spiritual brother Jesus. Jesus died by Roman crucifixion in 30 A.D. at the age of 35.

Jesus and John

Mark 1:4-9, 15; Matthew 3:7-11; Luke 3:16

About three years before Jesus started his full-time ministry, his cousin John began preaching in the wilderness near Jerusalem. Jesus would often visit John and talk with him about the meaning of the "Kingdom of God."[3]

John was no ordinary preacher and caused quite a stir with his odd lifestyle and clothing. To show his dedication to God alone, John left behind his life in the city and moved to the country to pray and preach at all times. He even left behind his clothes, and wore only a smock made of camel's hair. John ate whatever he could find, which often included insects and wild honey.

John urged the people to change their ways and to act as people who had had an authentic change-of-heart. Those who were willing to make a permanent change were baptized as a symbol of a new and changed life. John's favorite phrase, which he liked to repeat over-and-over, was "God's Kingdom is Coming! Prepare the way of the Lord!"

Some people began to think that John might be someone really special such as an ancient prophet resurrected from the dead, or perhaps an angel. To this, John replied, "Someone more powerful than I will succeed me. This person will be so great and so significant that I wouldn't even feel worthy to tie his shoe. I baptize with water, but he will baptize you with fire!"

Mark 1:10-11; Matthew 3:16; Luke 3:22; John 1:32

One day, Jesus appeared at one of John's baptismal services and requested baptism himself. John at first resisted, but at Jesus' urging, agreed to perform the baptism. For the rest of his life, John remembered this event and the way his heart felt warmed as he came out of the water with Jesus. It was on this day that any of his lingering doubts about his mission disappeared. A few months after this event, the illegitimate "King" of the Hebrews, Herod, had John thrown into prison for remarks he had made about Herod's wife. This would be the beginning of the end of John's short life.

Facing Doubts
Mark 1:12-13; Matthew 4:1-11; Luke 4:1-13

Jesus' official dedication to full-time ministry began with this baptism at the age of 31. He left his occupation as a carpenter in Nazareth and would spend the rest of his life serving God and the human race as a traveling teacher, healer, and visionary. But before he could begin, he knew that he had to face his own doubts and temptations. He set off to the barren desert alone for 40 days without food.

Well into his fast, Jesus felt the temptation to use spiritual power to satisfy his physical needs. The devil tormented him with a recurring plea: "Turn these stones to bread. Show your power!" To this Jesus responded, "Human beings are not to live on bread alone, but on every word that comes from the mouth of God." Then an even greater temptation manifested: "Prove you are truly favored by God by jumping off the highest floor of the temple in Jerusalem. All of the people of Jerusalem will see you being saved by the angels of God!" But Jesus calmly replied, "It is not proper to put the Lord to the test." These exchanges continued for days until Jesus knew the time was right. He exclaimed "Be gone Satan!" and the time for testing was over. His ministry had begun.

First Sermon
Matthew 5:3-6; Luke 6:20-23

Sometime after John's imprisonment, Jesus came to the area of Galilee in Northern Israel proclaiming God's good news. John the Baptist had preached of the coming Kingdom of God, but Jesus declared that it was now here! One of his first public sermons was along these lines:

> *Congratulations, you poor!*
> *The Kingdom of God belongs to you.*
> *Congratulations, you who are hungry!*
> *You will have an endless feast.*
> *Congratulations, you who now weep!*
> *You will know endless joy.*

Fishing for People

Mark 1:16-20; 2:14; Matthew 4:18-22; 9:9; Luke 5:27; John 1:35-51

One day, Jesus was walking along the Sea of Galilee and spotted Peter and his brother Andrew casting their fishing nets into the sea. He walked their direction until he was within earshot and then boldly proclaimed, "Become *my* followers and you will be fishing for people!" Something moved within Peter's heart and he abandoned his work immediately and followed Jesus. Andrew, also moved, followed close behind.

As they walked along together, talking, they caught sight of James (son of Zebedee) and John working on their nets. Right then and there, Jesus called out to them as well. James and John felt compelled to go where Jesus led and so told their father goodbye and followed Jesus.

Mark 1:16-20; 2:14; Matthew 4:18-22; 9:9; Luke 5:27; John 1:35-51

Sometime later, as Jesus was walking along, he came upon a toll booth. Manning the booth was a man named "Levi." Levi was a Jew who made his living collecting tolls for the Romans. Jesus looked him in the eye, smiled, and said, "Levi, come follow me." Levi left his toll booth and his occupation behind and followed Jesus.

Mark 1:29-42; 2:1-12; Luke 4:38-44

Once Jesus was visiting Peter's house when Peter's mother-in-law was sick with a high fever. Jesus touched her hand and the fever disappeared. She then got up and started doing some housework. Jesus' friends were becoming amazed at his wisdom and power.

Luke 17:20-21

Jesus spent a lot of time with his chosen friends doing God's work. At night, Jesus would talk to them about the Kingdom of God. One of his disciples asked, "When will the Kingdom of God arrive? When will it get here?" Jesus replied, "The Kingdom of God does not come by watching for it. You won't say 'Here it is!' or 'There it is over there!' No. The Kingdom of God is spread all over the earth, and yet, people do not see it. Therefore you will not be able to observe the 'coming' of the Kingdom of God. The Kingdom of God is here now, in your presence. It is within and among all of you."

Mark 9:50; Matthew 5:13

"Salt is good and makes food tasty. But what good is it of it becomes bland – if it looses its zing? With what will you make it salty again?"

Spreading the Word

Mark 1:23-39; Luke 4:33-43

One morning, very early, Jesus slipped away from where he was staying with his disciples and walked more than a mile to find a quiet place to meditate. When his friends woke up, and saw that he was not there, they became worried and began to search for him. After hours of searching they found him and with irritation Peter said, "Everyone has been looking for you!"

Calmly looking up from his prayer, Jesus paused and said, "It is time we moved on and spread our message. We are to go to the neighboring villages as they need our message as badly as this one does." So they went throughout the region of Galilee in Northern Israel, speaking in the churches and driving out demons.

Mark 1:23-39; Luke 4:33-43

At one of the churches they encountered a person with a particularly serious problem. The man had not been able to work in years, and often yelled uncontrollably and shouted obscenities. He was a danger to his family and friends. When the man caught sight of Jesus he screamed, "What are you doing here, Jesus of Nazareth? I know what you are! – A Holy Man of God!"

Jesus, unshaken, firmly responded, "Come out of him – now."

The man convulsed and let out an otherworldly ear-piercing shriek and then collapsed on the floor. For the first time in years he was free.

Instead of being thankful, some in the audience were afraid of *Jesus*! "What kind of man is this?," they exclaimed. So, with frequent occurrences such as this, Jesus' fame spread rapidly throughout Galilee and beyond.

Resisting Evil

Mark 1:21-22; Matthew 7:28-29; Luke 4:31-32; John 7:46

Jesus and his followers made their way to Capernaum, a town on the Northern shore of the Sea of Galilee. When Jesus arrived, he went directly to the town synagogue and began to teach. The audience was astonished at his teaching since he taught with authority instead of trying only to make a case for his ideas by quoting scripture.

Matthew 5:39-41; Luke 6:29-30

At one of his lectures, he addressed the audience as follows: "In your dealings with the world be as sly as snakes but as innocent as doves." "But, Teacher," a disciple replied, "how can we show love to those who are trying to hurt or kill us?" Jesus replied, "The best way to deal with violence is to not react violently to an evil person. In fact, if someone should slap you on the right cheek, give them your left as well. When you react to violence you get drawn into the violence and risk doing evil as well. If someone threatens to sue you for your coat, give them your coat and your shirt as well. And, even if the Roman officers force you to carry their goods an entire mile, then walk a second mile as well – all without anger. Do not feed the energy of a violent and evil person." "These sayings are hard to understand, and even harder to do," claimed another of Jesus' disciples, to which Jesus replied, "You must struggle to get in through the narrow door. Many will try to get in, but few will persevere. And I will tell you an even more difficult saying along these lines. Unless a person completely dedicates himself to the quest for God, that is, puts God ahead of all other relationships; mother, brother, sisters, he cannot be my true disciple."

Mark 1:29-42; 2:1-12; Luke 4:38-44

Once, Jesus was touring the countryside when a person with leprosy came up to him. The man fell to his knees pleading and begged Jesus, "Please make me well." Jesus seemed irritated, but stretched out his arm and touched him saying, "You are clean!" Immediately the leprosy disappeared and the man was completely well.

Mark 1:29-42; 2:1-12; Luke 4:38-44

Back in Capernaum, the word got around that Jesus was home. Many people crowded around so that there was no longer any room – even outside the door. Nevertheless, Jesus began to speak to them all. There were some people who showed up carrying their paralytic friend on a stretcher. Since they couldn't get in the door, they climbed up on the roof, removed some of the ceiling panels and began to lower their paralytic friend down to Jesus to be healed. When Jesus saw their simple faith and trust, he said (looking at the paralyzed man), "My child, your sins are forgiven." Some in the audience wondered to themselves, "Why does he say such things? Doesn't he know that only God can forgive sins?" Jesus sensed their doubts and addressed them: "Why are you entertaining such questions? Is it easier to say 'your sins are forgiven,' or 'pick up your mat and walk'?"

Then, the man got up, picked up his mat, and walked out as everyone looked on. Most of the crowd became ecstatic and spontaneously erupted in praise to God. One proclaimed, "We have never seen anything like this before!"

Eating with Sinners

Mark 2:15-17; Matthew 9:10-13; Luke 5:29-32

One time, Jesus was attending a large banquet. When he got his plate and sat down, he chose to sit in the section with the tax collectors and other people of bad reputation. When he got up again, a group of Pharisees pulled him aside and asked him to defend his odd behavior. "Why are you eating with those sinners?" they asked.

Jesus smiled and responded, "The able-bodied don't need a doctor, do they? It's the sick that do. I did not come to help the religious folk, but only the 'sinners.'" Despite his kind and well thought out answer, these Pharisees were still visibly perturbed and went on their way, scowling.

Mark 2:18-22; Matthew 9:14-15; Luke 5:33-34

On another occasion, a would-be disciple told Jesus that he was uncomfortable with the fact that Jesus didn't fast regularly as John the Baptist and the Pharisees did. Jesus answered, "The groom's friends do not fast while the groom is still around. You cannot expect them to fast when the celebration is still going on and they are all together enjoying one another's company. However the real issue is that people don't like to change their old customs and habits. Nobody wants to switch from their favorite food or drink that they have eaten all their life and try something new on a mere whim. People feel the same way about new ideas as they do new foods. They don't like change – sometimes to their great detriment.

Lord of the Sabbath

Mark 2:23-28; Matthew 12:1-8; Luke 6:1-5

One day, on their way back from the Synagogue on Saturday, Jesus and his disciples took a short-cut home through a field of grain. As they were hungry, they picked some of the heads of the grain and popped them in their mouths for a snack. Coming up behind them were some Pharisees who were annoyed at the disciples and Jesus. According to the Pharisees' interpretation of the Old

Testament, work was not allowed on the Sabbath and to them, picking a head of grain was "work." So they yelled ahead at Jesus, "Why do you allow your followers to break the laws of the Sabbath day?!"

Jesus said to them:

The Sabbath day was created *for* Humans;

Not humans for the Sabbath day.

The Sabbath day of worship was ordained to enlighten Mankind,

Not to be a senseless burden.

However, the Son of Man is Lord even over the Sabbath.

Mark 3:1-5; Matthew 12:9-13; Luke 6:6-10

That evening Jesus returned to the Synagogue and there met a man with a crippled hand. The Pharisees were still irritated about the incident earlier in the day, so they watched Jesus carefully to see if he would try and heal the man. They were hoping to get him on more "violations" of the Sabbath day-of-rest. To their surprise, Jesus announced loudly to the crippled man, "Come up here to the podium with me." Then he asked the audience, "Is it permissible to do good or evil on the Sabbath day? Is it better on the Sabbath day to save life or to destroy it?"

But the Pharisees stood their ground and did not reply. Jesus looked right at the Pharisees and said to the crippled man, "Hold out your hand!"

The man did as Jesus said and his hand become normal.

Good Things

Matthew 5:44-47; Luke 6:27-33

Jesus set up camp near the shoreline, and with a huge crowd gathering about him he began to teach. "Love your enemies. If you only love those who love you back, what does that prove? Even the worst of sinners love those who love them. And if you only do good things for people who do good things to you, what does that prove? Even the worst of sinners meet this minimum requirement."

And then he added, "God causes the sun to rise on both the bad and the good. Likewise he sends the rain to both the just and the unjust. Just look around you! God is generous to both the ungrateful and the wicked."

Matthew 7:9-11; Luke 11:11-13

He continued, "Would anyone among you hand your child a stone when he asked for bread? Would you hand him a snake if he was asking for a fish? Of course you wouldn't! If mere mortals, as unscrupulous as they are, still know how to give appropriate gifts to their children, isn't it even more likely that the Father in Heaven will give good things to those who ask of him?"

Mark 3:22-26; Matthew 12:24-36; Luke 11:15-23

Once, during one of his talks, a skeptic yelled, "He can drive out demons because he is league with Beelzebul, the prince of all demons!" Others would test him by demanding a sign from heaven. However, Jesus always knew what they were thinking, and he knew the heart of man. He responded to the neigh-sayers: "Any government that is divided within is soon devastated. A house divided soon falls. If Satan is divided, by attacking himself (supposedly through me), then how can his kingdom endure? Why would he do something not in his best interest? By the way, if I drive out demons in Beelzebul's name, in whose name do your people drive them out? Therefore, the character of those men will say a lot about your own motives. But what if I am really using the legitimate power of God? Wouldn't that be a clear signal that the Kingdom of God had arrived? I tell you this – I have started a wildfire on this earth; and I will guard it until it blazes."

Matthew 12:43-45; Luke 21:1-4

"When an unclean spirit leaves a person, it wanders through deserts looking for a place to rest. When it doesn't find one, it says to itself, 'I'll return to the place I left.' So it returns and finds the place swept and clean. Then it goes and finds its friends, who are even more evil, and they all settle into the comfortable arrangement. So you see, this person is even worse off then when he started."

Mark 3:27; Matthew 12:29; Luke 11:21-22

"No one can enter the house of a strong man and steal his things unless he first ties him up. Only then does the looting begin."

Growth

Mark 3:20-21;31-35; Matthew 12:46-50; Luke 8:19-21;
John 10:20

Jesus and his disciples traveled back to his hometown to get some rest and prepare for the next phase of his mission. They were staying in a house that belonged to one of Jesus' relatives. However, somehow word got out that Jesus was staying in town and desperate people began to crowd outside the house. Some folks were there to be healed. Some just wanted to see what this famous man, "Jesus," looked like. Others didn't like Jesus. They thought he was crazy and wanted him gone! So, the crowd was very rowdy. By the time Jesus' mother Mary arrived with his brothers James, Jude, Simon, and Joses, they could barely get to the front door. One of the disciples heard Mary's voice outside and told Jesus, "Sir. Your mother and brothers are here!"

In response, Jesus said, "Who are my mother and brothers?" And looking around the crowd of disciples in the house, making eye contact with each of them, he added, "Right here are my mother and brothers. Whoever thirsts for the Will of God – he or she is my brother, sister, or mother!"

Mark 4:1-8; Matthew 13:1-8; Luke 8:5-8

Returning to his encampment by the sea, he prepared to preach to the crowds. He got into a boat and sailed away from the shore, facing the growing throng. This day he would share with them several parables.

"A farmer went out to plant his seed. While he was sowing, some seed fell to the wayside and was eaten up by birds. Other seed fell upon the rocky soil and plants sprang right up. However, because the soil had no depth, and the roots were short, the plants were soon scorched to death by the sun. Some of the farmer's seed fell among the thorns. When the plants came up they were choked and produced no fruit. Finally, some of the seed fell on rich healthy soil and produced fruit. This seed sprouted and grew with a significant yield."

"Even when growing, growth is gradual. First someone plants a seed. Then the person checks its progress every day. The seed sprouts and then matures, although the farmer still cannot see it. Finally a tiny shoot is visible above the ground, then a head, then a fully mature plant. And when the grain is fully ripe the farmer gets his sickle because it is harvest time."

Kingdom of God

Matthew 22:2-13; Luke 14:15-24

Jesus liked to tell stories to illustrate spiritual truths. At one setting he shared the following parable: "A man was planning a big party and invited many guests. At 4:30pm, he sent his butler to tell the guests that the feast was ready. But one by one they made lame excuses why they couldn't come. Angered by the lack of appreciation, the man told his butler to go out in the streets and invite everyone. But even then, there were still seats available at the table. Then the man said: 'Invite everyone in the world; anyone who can walk or drag themselves to the party. I insist that my house be filled!'"

Mark 4:30-32; Matthew 13:31-32; Luke 13:18-19

"Let me tell you what the Kingdom of God is. It is like a small seed. Even though it is tiny, it becomes something great when it falls upon prepared soil. It grows into a large tree that becomes a shelter for the birds of the sky. Or one could say the Kingdom is like a small amount of yeast mixed into many pounds of dough. You cannot see its effects until the bread begins to rise."

"Or, the Kingdom of God is like a person who fantasized about murdering someone powerful. He thrust his sword into his wall at home – over and over – to see whether or not he had the strength to perform the nefarious deed.

Matthew 13:44

Later that day, Jesus said, "The Kingdom of God is like a valuable treasure hidden in a field. When someone finds it, they cover it back up and spend every cent they have to buy the field." And after a pause, he began again, "The Kingdom of Heaven is like a merchant who had a very large inventory and then came across a beautiful rare pearl. That merchant was wise; he sold everything he had…his entire inventory…to buy that single pearl."

Mark 6:10; Luke 10:5-8

Jesus gave the following advice to his apostles who were traveling to spread the Good News of the Kingdom of God: "When you enter a house, say, 'Peace to this house.' Stay at the one house and eat whatever food they are kind enough to provide. Don't complain and don't keep moving from house to house."

Mark 6:1-6; Matthew 13:54-58

Jesus left that place and traveled back to his hometown along with many of his disciples. On the Sabbath day, he went to the synagogue, as was his custom, and began to lecture. Many who heard were amazed at his insight and wisdom. "Where is he getting all this?" they would ask themselves. "I thought he was the son of a carpenter, a working class laborer?" And because of their prejudices and presuppositions, they had a hard time listening to him. Some in the crowd even acted resentful or jealous. Jesus stopped and addressed their doubt: "No prophet goes without respect except in his home country and among his relatives!" Because of the negative feelings he could not perform a single miracle there, except the curing of a few minor illnesses. He did travel all around the area though, and taught whomever would listen about the Kingdom of God.

Mark 5:24-34; Matthew 9:20-22; Luke 8:43-48

In one place where Jesus was staying, a large crowd gathered. So many wanted to be near him that it was difficult for him to walk. In the crowd was a desperate woman who had internal bleeding. The woman slowly worked her way through the throng and touched Jesus on the back, hoping for a miracle cure. When she touched him, she suddenly felt different inside. The bleeding had stopped the instant she touched Jesus and she was completely healed. Jesus stopped what he was doing, turned and looked at her and said, "Daughter, your faith has made you whole."

Wisdom's Children

Matthew 11:16-19; Luke 7:31-35

At one particular gathering, Jesus responded to some hecklers with the following lesson: "What is this world like? What is it *really* like? The people of this world are like little children at the park playing together and singing a song:

> We played the flute for you,
> but you wouldn't dance;
> then we sang a sad song,
> but you wouldn't cry.

My cousin John appeared in this world refusing fine foods and wine and you said he was 'too extreme.' But the Son of Man has not observed any particular dietary regimen and eats the same foods as his disciples and you say that he is a 'loose-liver' and a friend to scumbags and criminals. But I tell you, Wisdom is justified by her children."

Elijah Reborn

Mark 6:14-29; Matthew 14:1-12

News of Jesus' wisdom and teaching reached the ears of Herod the King. Many were saying that Jesus was the great Old Testament prophet Elijah reborn. Others thought he was the one to re-initiate the age of prophets that had ended with the great prophets 600 years before.

Earlier, King Herod had had John arrested and thrown into the dungeon. Herod's wife, Herodias, wanted John dead because he had preached publicly about the immorality of her divorce from her previous husband as well as Herod's mistreatment of his previous wife. However, deep down inside, Herod was afraid to kill John. Part of him wondered if John might actually be speaking for God, and if he were, if killing him might not bring God's curse.

On national holidays, Herod often threw elaborate parties for his wealthy friends and other high ranking officials. At one of these parties, his wife Herodias asked her daughter Salome to dance for the people there. Herod was so impressed with her show that he promised her up to half of his kingdom as a reward. He said this out loud in front of all his friends and supporters.

After consulting with her mother, Salome announced to the crowd, "I want John the Baptist's head delivered on a platter immediately!" Herod's jaw dropped in shock, but he realized that as King he could not back down after making such a bold promise in public. Herod glanced sadly to his left at his personal bodyguards and said, "Let it be done." Therefore, the guards notified the executioner and this evil deed was added to the other many evil deeds Herod had done.

Later, the news of John's death was brought to Jesus as he was preaching to a crowd. He shared the news of John's death and the mood became very sad. Then, after a long pause, Jesus announced, "When you went out to the wilderness to see John preach, what did you go to see? Grass blowing in the wind? What did you really go out to see? A man dressed in an expensive suit? But wait! Those who wear fine clothes are found in fancy buildings with a corner office."

Fruit

Mark 7:1-16; Matthew 15:10-11

Jesus was eating a large public meal with his disciples and friends. A group of Pharisees, who had heard rumors about Jesus, came to the meal in hopes of seeing what Jesus was like. Some of them wanted to see if they could catch him using a scriptural inaccuracy. Others among them were just curious. As they were mulling around, they noticed that some of the Jesus' disciples were eating without washing their hands. One of the Pharisees approached Jesus and questioned him directly, "Why aren't *your* disciples living up to the traditions of the elders? Why do you let them eat bread with defiled hands?" Now the Pharisaical tradition of hand washing had nothing to do with cleanliness. It was a ceremonial washing that they believed had been handed down by authoritative church leaders.

Jesus clapped him hands to get the attention of the crowd and addressed everyone on this matter: "Everyone listen, and please try hard to understand. It is not what goes into your body that defiles you. It is what comes out of your heart. Rituals can be useful, but they do not prove that a person's heart is pure. And the lack of them certainly does not prove that someone is unfit to worship God. There are those who ceremonially wash the outside of all of their cups. Why do they not also wash the inside? Wash the inside first. Then the outside will be clean as well."

"If you want to know what the heart of a person is really like, look at the fruit they produce. Good trees produce good fruit and bad trees produce bad fruit. People do not pick grapes from thorn trees or figs from thistles."

Do Unto Others

Mark 8:11-13; Matthew 12:38-40; 16:1-9; Luke 11:29-30

One time when Jesus was speaking to a crowd some members of the Pharisees were present. To test his authority one of them asked Jesus to cause a miraculous sign in the sky. With a frustrated look, Jesus replied, "Why does this generation insist on a sign? I solemnly promise, this generation won't get a sign!" Then Jesus simply turned around, walked back to his boat and crossed to the other side.

Mark 7:24-30; Matthew 15:21-28

Jesus then made his way to the seaside town of Tyre, which is just across the Northwestern-most border of Israel.

Jesus attempted to travel quietly so as to not be mobbed by the crowds. Nevertheless, a woman whose daughter had an unclean spirit managed, after great effort, to track him down. When she finally saw Jesus in person, she fell at his feet. This particular woman spoke Greek and not the native Aramaic tongue of Jesus. She was also a Phoenician by ethnicity who resided in Syria. The woman begged Jesus incessantly to heal her troubled daughter. Jesus said "Shouldn't the children be fed first? Is it fitting to take the bread from the children's mouths and throw it to the dogs?"

The woman replied, without missing a beat, "Even the dogs get to eat the scraps dropped by the children!"

Jesus then replied, "Because of your persistence and faith your daughter is healed. When you get home you will find her well."

When the woman got home she found her daughter fully recovered and sitting comfortably on the couch.

Mark 10:13-15; Matthew 18:3, 19:13-15; Luke 18:15-17

Frequently, parents would bring children to Jesus to receive a blessing. Jesus was fond of children and didn't seem to mind stopping what he was doing to spend time with them. Sometimes Jesus' adult friends would shoo the kids away, but Jesus corrected them: "Let the children come to me. Do not get in their way. You must realize that the Kingdom of God belongs to people just like that. In fact, if a person cannot accept God like a child does, they cannot really accept God at all."

Matthew 18:23-34

"The Kingdom of God can be compared to a high-ranking ruler who decided to settle accounts with his underlings. A debtor was brought to him who owed ten million dollars. Since he couldn't pay it back, the ruler ordered him to be sold into slavery along with his wife and children. In absolute desperation, the employee fell down on his knees before the ruler and begged, weeping, 'Be patient with me. I promise you, I will repay every cent.' Moved with compassion the ruler let the man go and completely cancelled his great debt. But, as soon as he was free, this same fellow who had received so much grace, saw one of his servants who owed him only 100 dollars, and grabbed him by the neck! He demanded, 'Pay me what you owe me if you value your life!' The servant begged for patience. But the employee who had received so much consideration by the ruler didn't even listen to the poor servant – in fact, he used his connections to have him thrown into debtor's prison. The other servants couldn't believe what they saw and word soon got back to the ruler. The employee who had owed the ten million dollars was summoned by the ruler once again. The ruler said, 'You wicked, wicked man! I showed you great compassion in forgiving your debt and yet you were harsh with this poor servant of yours. Shouldn't you have at least shown the same compassion to this man that you had received?' The ruler was so angry that he revoked the man's pardon and threw him in prison until his family could repay every last penny."

John 8:3-11

Jesus' lecture was interrupted by a gang of religious zealots. They approached Jesus, screaming and yelling that they had caught a woman in the act of adultery. The crowd cleared a path for them and they threw the woman at Jesus' feet. The man who brought her said, "Teacher, this woman was caught in the act of adultery. The Bible commands that such a woman should be pelted with stones until dead. What would you have us do?" Jesus' enemies said this in an attempt to trap him into breaking one of the technicalities in the religious law, but Jesus saw right through it.

Jesus stooped down and began drawing in sand with his finger. Everyone in the crowd anxiously awaited his words. After several minutes, Jesus stood up and proclaimed, "Whoever in this crowd has never committed a sin may throw the first stone." Again, he squatted on the ground and seemed to write with his finger.

The crowd began to slowly disperse. The oldest men in the crowd left first, but eventually everyone had gone leaving Jesus alone with the accused woman.

Jesus looked at her kindly and asked, "Where has everyone gone? Is there no one left to condemn you?"

She replied, "No one, sir."

"Then I do not do not condemn you either," Jesus said. "You are free to go, but, sin no more."

Riches

Luke 12:16-20; 18:24-25

It was widely believed during the time of Jesus that riches were a sign of God's favor. Jesus addressed this in one of his lectures. He began, "The rich are not any closer to God than anyone else. In fact, they have a very difficult time *entering* the Kingdom of God! I tell you the truth -- It is easier to thread a rope through the eye of a needle than it is for a rich person to enter God's domain. This is because no servant can be a slave to two masters. Without a doubt, the slave will hate one and love the other, or be devoted to one and disdain the other. You cannot serve both God and money."

Luke 12:16-20; 18:24-25

"Consider the following: There was a rich man who had a great deal of money. He said to himself, ' I shall invest my money so that I can fill my mansion and storehouse with stuff for me. Then I will use any extra to pad and protect my lifestyle. Nothing will hurt me!' But that very night he had a heart attack and died. None of the stuff he worked for went with him. He who has ears to hear should listen!"

Matthew 5:42; Luke 6:34

"If you have money to give, don't lend it at interest. Give it to someone from whom you will not get it back. If you only give money out of hope of gaining more, what merit it there in that? Even outlaws and sinners lend to their own if they can make a buck out of it."

Mark 8:35; Luke 17:33

"If you try to hang on to material life too tightly you will forfeit it, but, if you forfeit the transient material world you will live! Do not attach yourself to things which do not last."

Matthew 8:19-22; Luke 9:57-58

One day as Jesus and his followers were traveling down the road they came upon a group of men. One of the men listened carefully to Jesus and showed great interest in his cause. He said to Jesus, "I'll follow wherever you go!" Jesus replied to him, "Foxes have dens, and birds have nests; but the Son of Man has nowhere to rest his head." Then, to the group of men, Jesus simply said, "Follow me." But one of the men said, "I want to become your disciple, but I must wait until my Father dies; I have a responsibility to him as well." But Jesus said to him, "Let the dead bury their own dead; but *you* come and join me in announcing the Kingdom of God."

Your Neighbor

Mark 12:28-37; Matthew 22:34-40; Luke 10:25-28

On another occasion, a learned theologian of the Pharisee party sought out Jesus in sincerity and asked him the following heart-felt question: "Sir, I see you are a wise teacher, admired by the people. Of all the many commandments in the Old Testament, which one would you say was the most important of all?" Without missing a beat, Jesus replied by paraphrasing the Jewish "Shema" from the book of Deuteronomy: " 'Hear O Israel, the LORD our God is one LORD. And you shall love the LORD your God with all of your heart, and with all of your soul, with all of your mind, and all of your strength.' And the second greatest commandment is this, 'You shall love your neighbor as yourself.' There are no commandments in the entire Old Testament more important than these two. If you keep these, you will keep all of the others automatically. These commandments lead to eternal salvation." But the man did not give up so easily. He replied, "But sir, what do you mean by 'neighbor?'"

Jesus replied, "Consider this: A certain man was traveling from Jerusalem to Jericho. Unfortunately for him, robbers were hiding in the hills and they attacked him, took his belongings, and beat him nearly to death. They left his bruised and bloody body by the roadside. About 30 minutes after the robbery, a Priest came down the road. When he saw the man, he went way around him so that the man would not make him ritually 'unclean.' A little while later a temple assistant was coming down the road. He too saw the man, but didn't want to get involved. Finally a man from Samaria, a despised 'half-breed' Jew, was coming down the road. When he saw the poor beaten man he was moved with compassion. He ran to him and bandaged his wounds and treated them with medicine. Then he put the man on his own donkey and walked beside him all the way into town. He took him to a motel and paid the man's bill. He left some extra money at the front office, just in case the man needed it to get back on his feet. Now I ask you: Which of these three men in the story was a 'neighbor' to the injured man?" The learned Pharisee replied, "The one who showed him compassion." Jesus replied, "Go and do likewise."

Seeking

Mark 11:25-26; Matthew 6:7-15; 7:12; Luke 6:31; 11:1-4

Jesus prayed frequently and often sought out solitary places to pray. One time, one of his disciples asked him about the "secret" of prayer. Jesus responded: "When you pray, keep it simple. It isn't necessary to make a show or repeat long sentences." However, Jesus' followers insisted that he teach them a specific prayer to recite. "Alright – pray along these lines:

Great and Holy Father,
May you always be on our minds.
Give us our bread for today.
Bring about your Kingdom on Earth,
As it already is in Heaven.
Give us strength to forgive other people,
So that we may be at peace ourselves.
Amen.

If you sincerely want to be forgiven by God, then become a person of forgiveness. Practice forgiving others and you will thus find forgiveness yourself. And, when you pray, go into a room alone and shut the door behind you."

Luke 10:30-35

Jesus had been staying in the town of Jericho Ariha, which is East of Jerusalem near the Jordan river. As he was heading out of town, he noticed a blind beggar named Bartimaeus, sitting by the side of the road. As Jesus approached, Bartimaeus shouted with all his might, "Jesus, Son of David, have mercy on me!" Those around him told him to keep quiet, but he only shouted all the louder, "Son of David! Have mercy on me!" Jesus walked quickly to where the man was. When Jesus arrived, the man threw off his cloak and jumped to his feet. Jesus said, "What is it you want me to do for you?" The man answered, "Rabbi, I want to see again!" Jesus said to him, "You can now be on your way. Your faith has made you whole." And immediately he regained his sight and began to follow Jesus down the road.

Turning to the crowd, Jesus said, "People don't light a lamp and then put it under a basket. But rather, they put it upon a lamp stand where it can provide light for everyone around. And a giant city on the top of a mountain cannot be concealed."

Matthew 7:7-8; Luke 11:9-13

"Ask and it will be given you; seek, and you will find; knock on the door, and it will be opened for you. You can be sure that everyone who asks receives; everyone who seeks finds; and when a person knocks, the door is opened."

Matthew 7:1-5; Luke 6:37-42

After a pause he concluded, "There are those who see the speck of wood-dust in their friend's eye, but cannot see the log in their own eye! Take the log out of your eye and then you will see well enough to help your friend. Don't waste your energy judging other people. Work on the condition of your own heart. Remember – the standard you use to judge others will be the standard by which you yourself are judged."

Matthew 6:25-30; Luke 12:22-31

"Don't spend your energy worrying about life – what you are going to eat, or about clothing for your body. There is so much more to living than food and clothing. Think about the birds. They don't plant or harvest, nor do they have storehouses or barns. Yet God feeds them. Don't you realize that you are worth so much more than birds? God even knows the number of the hairs upon your head.

Can you add even one hour to your life by fretting about it? So if you can't even do that, why worry about anything? Think of the wildflowers. They neither worry nor sweat. Yet, even Solomon was never dressed as fine as them. If God so takes care of the plants in the field which are here today and gone tomorrow, is it not surely more likely that he has your best welfare in mind? Don't take anything for granted!"

Luke 13:6-9

Jesus then told the following parable: "A man had an apple tree planted in his backyard. He came out looking for fruit one day but couldn't find any apples on his tree. So he said to his gardener, 'I have been waiting three years for apples to grow on this tree. Cut it down! It is only wasting space in my backyard.' But the gardener replied, 'Sir. Please give it just one more year. I will work overtime on it with fertilizer, extra water, and care. I'll bet you anything it will produce some apples next year. But if not, I will cut it down then.'"

Matthew 18:12-13; Luke 15:4-9

Jesus posited the following question to a crowd: "If a woman has ten silver coins and misplaces only one of them, won't she keep searching until she finds it? In fact, she will frantically look in every corner of the house with her flashlight until the coin is found. Then the woman will call her friends to let them know the good news! "Celebrate with me," she will say, "the coin I lost has been found!"

If a shepherd owns a hundred sheep and only one of them wonders off, what will he do? He will leave the ninety nine at home and go looking for the little lost sheep. When he finds it, he we lift it up on him shoulders and smile. And, like the woman with the lost coin, he will call his friends to help him celebrate his discovery!"

Mark 10:31; Matthew 20:1-15

On one occasion, he opened his sermon with the words, "The last will be first and the first shall be last." He then went on to share this parable, "The Kingdom of Heaven is like a boss who went out at 7:00 A.M. to hire laborers for his farm. He agreed to pay them $50 for the days work, and sent them into the fields. At about 9:00 A.M. he went into town to visit the store and saw some young men bumming around outside. He told them that he had work for them and that he would pay them a fair wage to work his fields. They agreed and went back to the farm with him. He continued this process of going into town looking for laborers all day. Many men were hired. The last group joined the crew after 5:00 P.M. At 6:00 P.M., the whistle blew, and the men lined up to be paid. Everyone who worked that day received $50, one at a time. The men who worked all day were astonished! 'Why did you pay those guys who worked only an hour the same amount that you paid us?' The boss replied, 'I agreed to pay you $50, did I not? Did I wrong you? Isn't it my prerogative to pay my workers any wage I want? Your problem is that you are envious and jealous, when I am only trying to show generosity!'"

Luke 15:11-32

On a different occasion, he shared this parable:

Once there was a man with two teenage sons. The younger of the two came to his father and said, "Father. I am nearly an adult and ready to leave home and start my own life. Please give me my inheritance in advance." The father agreed and went ahead and divided a large amount of money between the two boys.

Not long after that, the younger son packed his things and left for the big city to find himself. But when he arrived he soon got in with the wrong crowd and behaved recklessly. Within six months he had spent his entire inheritance and had nothing to show for it. Unfortunately for him, just when he was approaching "rock bottom," the economy hit a terrible slump and there were no jobs available. In some places people couldn't even get enough to eat. He began to actually fear for his life and was overwhelmed with guilt. He finally managed to get a menial job as a pig-herder on the outskirts of the city. He became so hungry that he would sometimes steal some of the slop from the pigs and eat it himself.

Then one day, he came to his senses. He realized that even the servants that worked at his father's mansion had it better than he did! So he formulated a plan: "I will go to my father on my knees, and beg for his forgiveness. I will then pledge myself to him for life, as one of his servants." So the man stopped what he was doing and began the long journey back to his father's house.

While he was still far off in the distance, his father saw him coming. His heart melted at the sight of his lost son and he ran out to meet him. He threw his arms around his son and kissed him with joy. And with that, the prodigal son said, "Father, I have sinned against God and against you. I no longer deserve to be called your son. Please consider me as one of your servants."

However, the Father commanded his slaves, "Quickly! Get my finest coat and put it around his shoulders! Bring him my favorite gold ring from the top of my dresser! Tell the cooks to prepare our yearly feast early – today! We have something much more important to celebrate than the harvest! This son of mine was dead; but has come back to life. He was lost, but now he is found!" And everyone began to celebrate.

Now the older son, the one who had stayed and had been working daily for the Father, was out in the field working while all of this was going on. As he dragged his tired body home he heard music and dancing at the main house. He asked a servant boy what was going on.

The boy told him, "Your long lost brother is back! He has changed his ways and his heart! And, your father has thrown a great party to celebrate his return."

The older son grew angry and reused to go to the party. His father saw him outside pouting and went out to talk with him. He said to his father, "All these years I have slaved for you. I have been a good son. I have not wasted your money or disobeyed your orders. However, you have never once thrown a party for me. But when my deadbeat brother shows up you throw this feast!?"

To this the father replied, "My son; you have always been at my side. Everything that I have has been yours. But we *had* to celebrate! Your brother was *dead*, but he has come back to life. He was lost, but is now found."

Luke 16:1-8

"There once was a business owner whose Chief Executive Officer had been accused of squandering the owner's capital. The business' owner called him into his office and said, 'What is this I have heard about your behavior? I am ordering an audit of your files effective immediately. If things aren't on the up-and-up, you will be most certainly terminated!'

The C.E.O. was terrified. He thought to himself, 'What am I going to do? I have invested my life into this career. I am too proud to go on welfare.' So he began to formulate a plan. The C.E.O. called in each of the business owner's debtors. He said to the first, 'How much do you owe the company?' The man replied, 'Five thousand dollars.' The C.E.O. said to him, 'Here is your invoice – let's just make it $2,500 and call it even.' Then the C.E.O. called in another debtor who owed ten thousand dollars to the company. 'If you give me $8,000 today, I'll tear up your invoice." When word got back to the owner, he actually *praised* the dishonest C.E.O. for his shrewdness; for the children of this world in their time and place are wiser than the children of light.

Approaching Jerusalem

Matthew 6:6; Luke 18:9-14

Jesus began, "When you give to charity, don't let your left hand know what your right hand is doing. Give out of the overflow of your heart." However, his disciples prompted him for further explanation. He continued, "Consider the following: Two men went to church to pray. One was a high-ranking teacher of Moses' law; a Pharisee. The other was a despised tax collector – a traitor to his own people. The Pharisee prayed to God thus: 'I thank you God that I am not a sinner like everyone else. I thank you that I am not like that tax collector sitting there on the back pew. After all, I fast twice per week and always give a portion of my income to the church.'

But the tax collector sat all by himself and didn't even dare to look up at the altar. He beat his chest in despair and said 'Oh God, have mercy upon me – sinner that I am.'

I tell you the truth! The second man went home acquitted but the first did not! For those who promote themselves will be brought down, but those who demote themselves will be raised up. Consider this – in reality there is nothing now veiled that will not be eventually unveiled. There is nothing hidden that will not come to light. God sees the heart of man."

Mark 10:35-45; Luke 22:24-27; John 10:34; Psalm 82

As Jesus and his followers approached Jerusalem, James and John were discussing Jesus' coming kingdom among themselves. Finally, John worked up the courage to address Jesus directly. "When you come into your kingdom, can I sit at your right hand and James at your left? Can we be co-rulers with you in the coming kingdom?" Jesus replied, "You don't even know what you are asking! Do you *really* think you can walk with me all the way to the end? Do you really believe that you can also drink from this cup that I will have to drink from?" And with a loving pause and a shake of the head he continued, "Such things are not mine to give but belong to the Father alone." The others in the group overheard John's question and became very angry at his arrogance and secrecy. Jesus then addressed the entire group: "As you well know, those who rule this world do it with an iron hand. They believe that giving orders and having lots of followers are the measure of leadership. But they are wrong. If you want to be truly great then focus on serving others, not on giving orders. The greatest of all will be the one who is the servant of all. Let me be clear. I was not born so that I could be waited on hand-and-foot. Nor have I aspired to lead by force. In fact, before long, I will give my very life as a martyr: An example for many to follow. The spark of the divine rests in us all. Remember the psalm Asaph sang for the Lord (*Psalm 82*):

> *They know not, neither will they understand.*
> *They walk on in darkness:*
> *As the foundation of the Earth is out of course.*
> *I have said, "You all are gods,*
> *and children of the Sovereign Lord."*
> *But you all will die as mere men,*
> *The workers as well as the princes.*
> *Arise, O God. Judge this earth!*
> *Thy Kingdom Come!*

Mark 8:22-24

Jesus and his followers arrived in Bethsaida and Jesus began to teach. A blind man was brought to Jesus with the help of his friends. The blind man pleaded with Jesus to touch him and make him well. Jesus stopped what he was doing and took the blind man by the hand and led him out of the village. Jesus spat into the blind man's eyes, placed his hands on him and asked, "Do you see anything?" The man blinked and then squinted answering, "I see people walking around, I think. They look like trees." Jesus put his hand on the man's eyes again. The man strained to focus and then his expression changed. "Even the distant things are now clear," the man said.

John 5:2-9

In Jerusalem, by the Sheep Gate, there is a pool known as "Bethzatha" in the Hebrew language. It has five colonnades among which numerous handicapped people would gather. There was one man there who had been crippled for 38 years. Jesus saw him and realized that he had been there a long time. Jesus approached him and asked, "Do you want to get well?" The man replied, "Sir, I don't have anyone to put me in the pool when the water is agitated. Every time I try to make my way someone beats me to it." Moved with compassion Jesus responded, "Get up, pick up your mat and walk." The man recovered at once and picked up his mat as Jesus said.

Mark 11:15-17; Matthew 19:45-46; 21:12-13

Jesus and his followers arrived in Jerusalem for the last time. As planned, he showed up at the temple and made a bold statement by driving out the money changers and sellers in the temple. He addressed them directly in front of the crowds, "The scriptures say, *'Mine house shall be called a house of prayer for all people,'* but you have turned it into a den of thieves!"

Mark 12:13-17

Jesus' actions in Jerusalem led to many public disputes with community leaders. Once, they showed Jesus a gold coin and said to him, "The Roman government demands taxes from us." Jesus replied, "Give to the emperor what belongs to the emperor, and give to God what belongs to God.

Mark 4:25; Matthew 25:14-28; Luke 19:13-27

On another occasion he began his sermon with these words: "Those who have will be given more; those who have nothing will be deprived of even the little they have."

He then explained himself using a parable. "A man of importance was planning a business trip and called his employees into the office. He told them he needed them to look over his financial interests while he was out of town. To the first employee he gave a check for $20,000. To the second employee he gave a check for $8,000. And to a third employee he gave a check for $4,000. Each check was given in relation to the ability of the person who received it.

The man who had received $20,000 immediately went to work on his plan. Within a short time he had $40,000. The man who had been entrusted with $8,000 also doubled his money and now had $16,000. However, the third man hid his entire $4,000 in a pillow case and placed it at the bottom of his closet.

After a long absence, the boss returned to see how his investments were doing. He called the first man into his office, and the man reported, 'Sir, you entrusted me with $20,000 and I have turned it into $40,000.' 'Well done, my man!' said the boss. 'Because of your hard work I will make you a partner in the firm. You have shown that you can handle the responsibility.' The man who had been entrusted with $8000 also came and reported, 'I have doubled your money!' 'Well done! From now on I will trust you with even larger sums of money.'

But then, the man who had been given the smallest amount of money came forward. 'Sir,' he stuttered, 'You are an important man who takes whatever he wants and pushes people to their absolute limits. I was afraid of what you might do to me if I failed, so I hid your money in my closet. I didn't risk doing *anything* with it. Here is your $4000 back.' The boss angrily replied to him: 'You useless wimp! So you were afraid of me, were you? Then you should have done something with the money. At the very least, you could have put it in a savings account and earned a little interest. Take this fellow's money away and give it to the one with $40,000! Now get out of my sight!'

Mark 12:1-8; 14:1-7; Luke 7:36-39

Jesus arrived in Bethany just outside of Jerusalem. He lodged in the house of Simon the leper and was sitting down to eat dinner. One of the women at the dinner presented Jesus with some very costly perfume which she poured over his head as a sign of her respect for him. Some of the other guests were angry at the woman's actions. They felt that the anointing of Jesus' head was a waste of money that could have been used for charitable purposes. The woman could feel the dirty looks from the other guests. But, knowing their thoughts, Jesus said, "Why are you holding a grudge against this woman? Her intentions were pure and she has done something truly good and honorable. For you will always have the poor with you and you can do good to them whenever you feel like it. However, I will not be here much longer."

Later he shared this story with them: "A person owned a vineyard and rented it to some farmers so that they collect the crop for him. After a while he sent one of his slaves to the vineyard to collect the profits. But the farmers grabbed the slave, beat him almost to death and sent him back to the owner of the vineyard. The owner thought to himself, 'Perhaps these men made a mistake. Maybe they didn't realize that it was *my* slave.' So he sent another slave with an official seal. However, the farmers beat this slave as well. So the owner said to himself, 'I will send my son. Surely they will show respect for him.' But when the owner's son showed up at the vineyard, they grabbed him and beat him to death; knowing he was the rightful heir to the vineyard."

The Passion
Mark 14:43-15:37; Luke 22:52-53; John 18:2-12;
I Corinthians 15:8

Near nightfall, Jesus and his Disciples camped at a place called "Gethsemane, " just outside of Jerusalem. Feeling sorrowful, Jesus walked into the woods to pray. He asked Peter, James, and John to come with him.

Having been led by one of Jesus' disciples, the police showed up where Jesus and his friends were gathered. The police seized Jesus and held him tightly. One of Jesus' disciples took out his sword to defend him, but Jesus ordered him to put it back. "Do you not know that all those who live by the sword, die by the sword?"

Terrified, the rest of the disciples fled as fast as they could, leaving Jesus alone. Eventually Jesus was brought before the High Priest – the religious authority of the Jewish Nation.

The Priest had Jesus turned over to the secular ruler of the region, Pontius Pilate. Pilate had Jesus flogged with a whip and then ordered that he be crucified.

Roman soldiers brought him to a place called "Golgotha," which in English is translated "The Place of the Skull or 'Calvary.'" And Jesus was crucified there.

As he hung from the cross, in visible anguish, he recited Psalms for comfort as was the custom of the Jews. He could be heard quoting the 22nd Psalm, "My God, My God, why hast thou forsaken me? Why art thou so far from helping me, and from the words of my groaning?" [4]

There were some women observing from a distance among whom were Mary Magdalene, James mother - Mary, as well as the mother of James the Younger and Joses. Salome was also there.

These were the women that had been with him all along and assisted in his ministry and accompanied him to Jerusalem. As they looked upon Jesus' body they saw him take his last breath.

Mark 14:43-15:37; Luke 22:52-53; John 18:2-12;
I Corinthians 15:8

Although it looked like the end, about three days later, Jesus appeared to Mary Magdalene, the woman from whom he had driven out seven demons. Mary ran to tell the other disciples, whom she found huddled together in a room, mourning and weeping. When Mary told the group that that she had seen Jesus, they did not believe her as they were absorbed in deep sorrow.[5]

Later, Christ appeared to Peter and many others at a previously decided location in Galilee.[6]

The organized church began in Jerusalem and was headed by Jesus' brother, James, and Peter, as well as John Zebedee.

Later, Paul of Tarsus also had a vision of the risen Jesus.

4

The Story in Topical Order

Following is an organized arrangement of the major topics covered in the teachings of the Historical Jesus. They are presented in the order and magnitude in which they were stressed by the reconstructed "Yeshua Barnasha;" the proposed Historical Jesus of this project. In this topical presentation, only Jesus' words are included. Following this topical presentation will be the section of the book which presents Jesus' sayings in a Catechismal format.

Karma

Karma is the cosmic principle of cause and effect. The idea that all actions, whether good or evil, must run their natural course. All actions involving others must also be experienced by the doer. Thus, the only way to improve one's situation is to modify the way one acts and chooses. We are completely responsible for our outcomes and states.

Mark 4:25; Matthew 25:14-28; Luke 19:13-27

Those who have will be given more; those who have nothing will be deprived of even the little they have.

A man of importance was planning a business trip and called his employees into the office. He told them he needed them to look over his financial interests while he was out of town. To the first employee he gave a check for $20,000. To the second employee he gave a check for $8,000. And to a third employee he gave a check for $4,000. Each check was given in relation to the ability of the person who received it. The man who had received $20,000 immediately went to work on his plan. Within a short time he had $40,000. The man who had been entrusted with $8,000 also doubled his money and now had $16,000. However, the third man hid his entire $4,000 in a pillow case and placed it at the bottom of his closet. After a long absence, the boss returned to see how his investments were doing. He called the first man into his office, and the man reported, 'Sir, you entrusted me with $20,000 and I have turned it into $40,000.' 'Well done, my man!' said the boss. 'Because of your hard work I will make you a partner in the firm. You have shown that you can handle the responsibility.' The man who had been entrusted with $8000 also came and reported, 'I have doubled your money!' 'Well done! From now on I will trust you with even larger sums of money.' But then, the man who had been given the smallest amount of money came forward. 'Sir,' he stuttered, ' You are an important man who takes whatever he wants and pushes people to their absolute limits. I was afraid of what you might do to me if I failed, so I hid your money in the ground. I didn't risk doing *anything* with it. Here is your $4000 back.' The boss angrily replied to him:

'You useless wimp! So you were afraid of me, were you? Then you should have done something with the money. At the very least, you could have put it in a savings account and earned a little interest. Take this fellow's money away and give it to the one with $40,000! Now get out of my sight!'

Mark 7:1—16; Matthew 15:10-11

Everyone listen, and please try hard to understand. It is not what goes into your body that defiles you. It is what comes out of your heart. Rituals can be useful, but they do not prove that a person's heart is pure. And the lack of them certainly does not prove that someone is unfit to worship God. There are those who ceremonially wash the outside of all of their cups. Why do they not also wash the inside? Wash the inside first. Then the outside will be clean as well.

If you want to know what the heart of a person is really like, look at the fruit they produce. Good trees produce good fruit and bad trees produce bad fruit. People do not pick grapes from thorn trees or figs from thistles.

Mark 11:25-26; Matthew 6:7-15; 7:12; Luke 6:31; 11:1-4

If you sincerely want to be forgiven by God, then become a person of forgiveness. Practice forgiving others and you will thus find forgiveness yourself. And, when you pray, go into a room alone and shut the door behind you.

Matthew 6:6; Luke 18:9-14

Two men went to church to pray. One was a high-ranking teacher of Moses' law; a Pharisee. The other was a despised tax collector – a traitor to his own Jewish people. The Pharisee prayed to God thus: 'I thank you God that I am not a sinner like everyone else. I thank you that I am not like that tax collector sitting there on the back pew. After all, I fast twice per week and always give a portion of my income to the church.'

But the tax collector sat all by himself and didn't even dare to look up at the altar. He beat his chest in despair and said 'Oh God, have mercy upon me – sinner that I am.' I tell you the truth! The second man went home acquitted but the first did not! For those who promote themselves will be brought down, but those who demote themselves will be raised up.

Consider this – in reality there is nothing now veiled that will not be eventually unveiled. There is nothing hidden that will not come to light. God sees the heart of man.

Matthew 7:1-5; Luke 6:37-42

There are those who see the speck of wood-dust in their friend's eye, but cannot see the log in their own eye! Take the log out of your eye and then you will see well enough to help your friend. Don't waste your energy judging other people. Work on the condition of your own heart. Remember – the standard you use to judge others will be the standard by which you yourself are judged.

Mark 14:43-15:37; Luke 22:52-53; John 18:2-12; I Corinthians 15:8

Do you not know that all those who live by the sword, die by the sword?

Matthew 7:7-8; Luke 11:9-13

Ask and it will be given you; seek, and you will find; knock on the door, and it will be opened for you. You can be sure that everyone who asks receives; everyone who seeks finds; and when a person knocks, the door is opened.

Mark 4:1-8; Matthew 13:1-8; Luke 8:5-8

A farmer went out to plant his seed. While he was sowing, some seed fell to the wayside and was eaten up by birds. Other seed fell upon the rocky soil and plants sprang right up. However, because the soil had no depth, and the roots were short, the plants were soon scorched to death by the sun. Some of the farmer's seed fell among the thorns. When the plants came up they were choked and produced no fruit. Finally, some of the seed fell on rich healthy soil and produced fruit. This seed sprouted and grew with a significant yield.

Even when growing, growth is gradual. First someone plants a seed. Then the person checks its progress every day. The seed sprouts and then matures, although the farmer still cannot see it. Finally a tiny shoot is visible above the ground, then a head, then a fully mature plant. And when the grain is fully ripe the farmer gets his sickle because it is harvest time.

John 8:3-11

To the woman caught in the act of adultery who narrowly escaped being put to death: "Where has everyone gone? Is there no one left to condemn you?" She replied, "No one, sir."

"Then I do not do not condemn you either," Jesus said. "You are free to go, but sin no more."

Matthew 6:6; Luke 18:9-14

When you give to charity, don't let your left hand know what your right hand is doing. Give out of the overflow of your heart.

Mark 12:28-37; Matthew 22:34-40; Luke 10:25-28

A certain man was traveling from Jerusalem to Jericho. Unfortunately for him, robbers were hiding in the hills and they attacked him, took his belongings, and beat him nearly to death. They left his bruised and bloody body by the roadside. About 30 minutes after the robbery, a Priest came down the road. When he saw the man, he went way around him so that the man would not make him ritually 'unclean.' A little while later a temple assistant was coming down the road. He too saw the man, but didn't want to get involved. Finally a man from Samaria, a despised 'half-breed' Jew, was coming down the road. When he saw the poor beaten man he was moved with compassion. He ran to him and bandaged his wounds and treated them with medicine. Then he put the man on his own donkey and walked beside him all the way into town. He took him to a motel and paid the man's bill. He left some extra money at the front office, just in case the man needed it to get back on his feet. Now I ask you: Which of these three men in the story was a 'neighbor' to the injured man?

Matthew 18:23-34

The Kingdom of God can be compared to a high-ranking ruler who decided to settle accounts with his underlings. A debtor was brought to him who owed ten million dollars. Since he couldn't pay it back, the ruler ordered him to be sold into slavery along with his wife and children. In absolute desperation, the employee fell down on his knees before the ruler and begged, weeping, "Be patient with me. I promise you, I will repay every cent." Moved with compassion the ruler let the man go and completely cancelled his great debt. But, as soon as he was free, this same fellow who had received so much grace, saw one of his servants who owed him only 100 dollars, and grabbed him by the neck! He demanded, "Pay me what you owe me if you value your life!" The servant begged for patience. But the employee who had received so much consideration by the ruler didn't even listen to the poor servant – in fact, he used his connections to have him thrown into debtor's prison. The other servants couldn't believe what they saw and word soon got back to the ruler. The employee who had owed the ten million dollars was summoned by the ruler once again. The ruler said, "You wicked, wicked man! I showed you great compassion in forgiving your debt and yet you were harsh with this poor servant of yours. Shouldn't you have at least shown the same compassion to this man that you had received?" The ruler was so angry that he revoked the man's pardon and threw him in prison until his family could repay every last penny.

Matthew 5:39-41; Luke 6:29-30

The best way to deal with violence is to not react violently to an evil person. In fact, if someone should slap you on the right cheek, give them your left as well. When you react to violence you get drawn into the violence and risk doing evil as well. If someone threatens to sue you for your coat, give them your coat and your shirt as well. And, even if the Roman officers force you to carry their goods an entire mile, then walk a second mile as well – all without anger. Do not feed the energy of a violent and evil person.

You must struggle to get in through the narrow door. Many will try to get in, but few will persevere. And I will tell you an even more difficult saying along these lines. Unless a person completely dedicates himself to the quest for God, that is, puts God ahead of all other relationships; mother, brother, sisters, he cannot be my disciple.

Matthew 12:43-45; Luke 21:1-4

When an unclean spirit leaves a person, it wanders through deserts looking for a place to rest. When it doesn't find one, it says to itself, "I'll return to the place I left." So it returns and finds the place swept and clean. Then it goes and finds its friends, who are even more evil, and they all settle into the comfortable arrangement. So you see, this person is even worse off then when he started.

Mark 11:25-26; Matthew 6:7-15; 7:12; Luke 6:31; 11:1-4

When you pray, keep it simple. It isn't necessary to make a show or repeat long sentences.

Pray along these lines: *Great and Holy Father, may you always be on our minds. Give us our bread for today. Bring about your Kingdom on Earth, as it already is in Heaven. Give us strength to forgive other people, So that we may be at peace ourselves. Amen.*

Luke 13:6-9

A man had an apple tree planted in his backyard. He came out looking for fruit one day but couldn't find any apples on his tree. So he said to his gardener, "I have been waiting three years for apples to grow on this tree. Cut it down! It is only wasting space in my backyard." But the gardener replied, "Sir. Please give it just one more year. I will work overtime on it with fertilizer, extra water, and care. I'll bet you anything it will produce some apples next year. But if not, I will cut it down then."

Mark 12:28-37; Matthew 22:34-40; Luke 10:25-28

A religious leader asks Jesus which commandment is the most important:

Hear O Israel, the LORD our God is one LORD. And you shall love the LORD your God with all of your heart, and with all of your soul, with all of your mind, and all of your strength.' And the second greatest commandment is this, 'You shall love your neighbor as yourself.' There are no commandments in the entire Old Testament more important than these two. If you keep these, you will keep all of the others automatically. These commandments lead to eternal salvation.

Mark 10:35-45; Luke 22:24-27; John 10:34; Psalm 82

Those who rule this world do it with an iron hand. They believe that giving orders and having lots of followers are the measure of leadership. But they are wrong. If you want to be truly great then focus on serving others, not on giving orders. The greatest of all will be the one who is the servant of all. Let me be clear. I was not born so that I could be waited on hand-and-foot. Nor have I aspired to lead by force. If fact, before long, I will give my very life as a martyr: an example for many to follow. The spark of the divine rests in us all.

Remember the psalm Asaph sang for the Lord (Psalm 82): *They know not, neither will they understand. They walk on in darkness, as the foundation of the Earth is out of course. I have said, "You all are gods, and children of the Sovereign Lord." But you all will die as mere men, the workers as well as the princes. Arise, O God. Judge this earth! Thy Kingdom come!*

Matthew 5:39-41; Luke 6:29-30

In your dealings with the world be as sly as snakes but as innocent as doves.

Mark 3:27; Matthew 12:29; Luke 11:21-22

No one can enter the house of a strong man and steal his things unless he first ties him up. Only then does the looting begin.

Mark 2:23-28; Matthew 12:1-8; Luke 6:1-5

The Sabbath day was created *for* Humans; not humans for the Sabbath day. The Sabbath day of worship was ordained to enlighten Mankind, not to be a senseless burden. However, the Son of Man is Lord even over the Sabbath.

Mark 5:24-34; Matthew 9:20-22; Luke 8:43-48

Daughter, your faith has made you whole.

Luke 10:30-35

People don't light a lamp and then put it under a basket. But rather, they put it upon a lamp stand where it can provide light for everyone around. And a giant city on the top of a mountain cannot be concealed.

Mark 12:1-8; 14:1-7; Luke 7:36-39

For you will always have the poor with you and you can do good to them whenever you feel like it.

A person owned a vineyard and rented it to some farmers so that they collect the crop for him. After a while he sent one of his slaves to the vineyard to collect the profits. But the farmers grabbed the slave, beat him almost to death and sent him back to the owner of the vineyard. The owner thought to himself, "Perhaps these men made a mistake. Maybe they didn't realize that it was *my* slave." So he sent another slave with an official seal. However, the farmers beat this slave as well. So the owner said to himself, "I will send my son. Surely they will show respect for him." But when the owner's son showed up at the vineyard, they grabbed him and beat him to death; knowing he was the rightful heir to the vineyard.

Kingdom of God

In the Judeo-Christian scriptures, the Kingdom of God is defined almost entirely by parable. It is represented as the idealized dwelling of God and his people as well as a future state-of-being. The Kingdom of God is closely associated with spiritual rebirth.

Mark 1:4-9, 15; Matthew 3:7-11; Luke 3:16

Jesus would often visit John and talk with him about the meaning of the "Kingdom of God."

Mark 4:30-32; Matthew 13:31-32; Luke 13:18-19

Let me tell you what the Kingdom of God is. It is like a small seed. Even though it is tiny, becomes something great when it falls upon prepared soil. It grows into a large tree that becomes a shelter for the birds of the sky. Or one could say the Kingdom is like a small amount of yeast mixed into many pounds of dough. You cannot see its effects until the bread begins to rise.

Luke 17:20-21

The Kingdom of God is spread all over the earth, and yet, people do not see it. Therefore you will not be able to observe the "coming" of the Kingdom of God. The Kingdom of God is here now, in your presence. It is within and among all of you.

Mark 10:13-15; Matthew 18:3, 19:13-15; Luke 18:15-17

Let the children come to me. Do not get in their way. You must realize that the Kingdom of God belongs to people just like that. In fact, if a person cannot accept God like a child does, they cannot really accept God at all.

Matthew 13:44

The Kingdom of God is like a valuable treasure hidden in a field: when someone finds it, they cover it back up and spend every cent they have to buy the field. The Kingdom of Heaven is like a merchant who had a very large inventory and then came across a beautiful rare pearl. That merchant was wise; he sold everything he had...all of his inventory... to buy that single pearl.

Mark 10:35-45; Luke 22:24-27; John 10:34; Psalm 82

As you well know, those who rule this world do it with an iron hand. They believe that giving orders and having lots of followers are the measure of leadership. But they are wrong. If you want to be truly great then focus on serving others, not on giving orders. The greatest of all will be the one who is the servant of all. Let me be clear. I was not born so that I could be waited on hand-and-foot. Nor have I aspired to lead by force. If fact, before long, I will give my very life as a martyr: an example for many to follow. The spark of the divine rests in us all.

Matthew 7:1-5; Luke 6:37-42

Don't waste your energy judging other people. Work on the condition of your own heart. Remember – the standard you use to judge others will be the standard by which you yourself are judged.

Luke 10:30-35

People don't light a lamp and then put it under a basket. But rather, they put it upon a lamp stand where it can provide light for everyone around. And a giant city on the top of a mountain cannot be concealed.

Mark 10:35-45; Luke 22:24-27; John 10:34; Psalm 82

Remember the psalm Asaph sang for the Lord (Psalm 82): *They know not, neither will they understand. They walk on in darkness, as the foundation of the Earth is out of course. I have said, "You all are gods, and children of the Sovereign Lord." But you all will die as mere men; the workers as well as the princes. Arise, O God. Judge this earth! Thy Kingdom come!*

Mark 12:13-17

Give to the emperor what belongs to the emperor, and give to God what belongs to God.

Mark 14:43-15:37; Luke 22:52-53; John 18:2-12;
I Corinthians 15:8

Do you not know that all those who live by the sword, die by the sword?

Luke 16:1-8

There once was a business owner whose Chief Executive Officer had been accused of squandering the owner's capital. The business' owner called him into his office and said, "What is this I have heard about your behavior? I am ordering an audit of your files effective immediately. If things aren't on the up-and-up, you will be most certainly terminated!"

The C.E.O. was terrified. He thought to himself, "What am I going to do? I have invested my life into this career. I am too ashamed to go on welfare.' So he began to formulate a plan.

The C.E.O. called in each of the business owner's debtors. He said to the first, "How much do you owe the company?" The man replied, "Five thousand dollars." The C.E.O. said to him, "Here is your invoice – let's just make it $2,500 and call it even."

Then the C.E.O. called in another debtor who owed ten thousand dollars to the company. "If you give me $8,000 today, I'll tear up your invoice." When word got back to the owner, he actually *praised* the dishonest C.E.O. for his shrewdness; for the children of this world in their time and place are wiser than the children of light.

Matthew 6:6; Luke 18:9-14

Two men went to church to pray. One was a high-ranking teacher of Moses' law; a Pharisee. The other was a despised tax collector – a traitor to his own Jewish people. The Pharisee prayed to God thus: "I thank you God that I am not a sinner like everyone else. I thank you that I am not like that tax collector sitting there on the back pew. After all, I fast twice per week and always give a portion of my income to the church." But the tax collector sat all by himself and didn't even dare to look up at the altar. He beat his chest in despair and said "Oh God, have mercy upon me – sinner that I am." I tell you the truth! The second man went home acquitted but the first did not! For those who promote themselves will be brought down, but those who demote themselves will be raised up.

Consider this – in reality there is nothing now veiled that will not be eventually unveiled. There is nothing hidden that will not come to light. God sees the heart of man.

Mark 11:15-17; Matthew 19:45-46; 21:12-13

The scriptures say, *"Mine house shall be called a house of prayer for all people,"* but you have turned it into a den of thieves!

Mark 1:4-9, 15; Matthew 3:7-11; Luke 3:16

John the Baptist when questioned about the advent of Jesus: This person will be so great and so significant that I wouldn't even feel worthy to tie his shoe. I baptize with water, but he will baptize you with fire!

Mark 4:30-32; Matthew 13:31-32; Luke 13:18-19; Gospel of Thomas

The Kingdom of God is like a person who fantasized about murdering someone powerful. He thrust his sword into his wall at home – over and over – to see whether or not he had the strength to perform the nefarious deed.

Matthew 11:16-19; Luke 7:31-35

What is this world like? What is it *really* like? The people of this world are like little children at the park playing together and singing a song: "We played the flute for you, but you wouldn't dance; then we sang a sad song, but you wouldn't cry." My cousin John appeared in this world refusing fine foods and wine and you said he was "too extreme." But the Son of Man has not observed any particular dietary regimen and eats the same foods as his disciples and you say that he is a "loose-liver," and a friend to scumbags and criminals. But I tell you, Wisdom is justified by her children.

Matthew 18:12-13; Luke 15:4-9

If a woman has ten silver coins and misplaces only one of them, won't she keep searching until she finds it? In fact, she will frantically look in every corner of the house with her light until the coin is found. Then the woman will call her friends to let them know the good news! "Celebrate with me," she will say, "the coin I lost has been found!"

Luke 15:11-32

Once there was a man with two teenage sons. The younger of the two came to his father and said, "Father. I am nearly an adult and ready to leave home and start my own life. Please give me my inheritance in advance." The father agreed and went ahead and divided a large amount of money between the two boys.

Not long after that, the younger son packed his things and left for the big city to find himself. But when he arrived he soon got in with the wrong crowd and behaved recklessly. Within six months he had spent his entire inheritance and had nothing to show for it. Unfortunately for him, and just when he was approaching "rock bottom," the economy hit a terrible slump and there were no jobs available. In some places people couldn't even get enough to eat. He began to actually fear for his life and was overwhelmed with guilt. He finally managed to get a menial job as a pig-herder on the outskirts of the city. He became so hungry that he would sometimes steal some of the slop from the pigs and eat it himself.

Then one day, he came to his senses. He realized that even the servants that worked at his father's mansion had it better than he did! So he formulated a plan: "I will go to my father on my knees, and beg for his forgiveness. I will then pledge myself to him for life, as one of his servants." So the man stopped what he was doing and began the long journey back to his father's property.

While he was still far off in the distance his father saw him coming. His heart melted at the sight of his lost son and he ran out to meet him. He threw his arms around his son and kissed him with joy. And with that, the prodigal son said, "Father, I have sinned against God and against you. I no longer deserve to be called your son. Please consider me as one of your servants."

However, the Father commanded his slaves, "Quickly! Get my finest coat and put it around his shoulders! Bring him my favorite gold ring from the top of my dresser! Tell the cooks to prepare our yearly feast early – today! We have something much more important to celebrate than the harvest! This son of mine was dead; but has come back to life. He was lost, but now he is found!" And everyone began to celebrate.

Now the older son, the one who had stayed and had been working daily for the father, was out in the field working while all of this was going on. As he dragged his tired body home he heard music and dancing at the main house. He asked a servant boy what was going on.

The boy told him, "Your long lost brother is back! He has changed his ways and his heart! And, your father has thrown a great party to celebrate his return."

The older son grew angry and reused to go to the party. His father saw him outside pouting and went out to talk with him. He said to his father, "All these years I have slaved for you. I have been a good son. I have not wasted your money or disobeyed your orders. However, you have never once thrown a party for me. But when my deadbeat brother shows up you throw this feast!?"

To this the father replied, "My son; you have always been at my side. Everything that I have has been yours. But we *had* to celebrate! Your brother was *dead*, but he has come back to life. He was lost, but is now found."

Mark 4:1-8; Matthew 13:1-8; Luke 8:5-8

A farmer went out to plant his seed. While he was sowing, some seed fell to the wayside and was eaten up by birds. Other seed fell upon the rocky soil and the plants sprang right up. However, because the soil had no depth, and the roots were short, the plants were soon scorched to death by the sun. Some of the farmer's seed fell among the thorns. When the plants came up they were choked and produced no fruit. Finally, some of the seed fell on rich healthy soil and produced fruit. This seed sprouted and grew with a significant yield.

Even when growing, growth is gradual. First someone plants a seed. Then the person checks its progress every day. The seed sprouts and then matures, although the farmer still cannot see it. Finally a tiny shoot is visible above the ground, then a head, then a fully mature plant. And when the grain is fully ripe the farmer gets his sickle because it is harvest time.

Luke 18:2-5

Here is another example. Once there was a powerful judge. He lived in a small town where he was familiar to the townspeople. He prided himself on being a "self-made man." He wasn't particularly religious, and had no patience for people who wasted his time. In the same town, there was a widow who came to his office just about every week and demanded: "Please consider my case against this person I am suing!"

For a long time the judge resisted. The case just didn't seem important enough to warrant his attention. However, the widow's persistence at last wore him down. He said to himself, " I am afraid of nothing, and no one. However, I am going to help this woman just so that she will go away and stop pestering me!" Such is the way of this world. Even though the judge has no genuine compassion for the woman, he eventually helped her because of her persistence.

Matthew 6:6; Luke 18:9-14

When you give to charity, don't let your left hand know what your right hand is doing. Give out of the overflow of your heart.

Luke 10:30-35

Your faith has made you whole.

Mark 9:50; Matthew 5:13

Salt is good and makes food tasty. But what good is it of it becomes bland – if it looses its zing? With what will you make it salty again?

God's Nature

The character of God contrasted against the proclivities of humankind.

Matthew 5:44-47; Luke 6:27-33

Love your enemies. If you only love those who love you back, what does that prove? Even the worst of sinners love those who love them. And if you only do good things for people who do good things to you, what does that prove? Even the worst of sinners meet this minimum requirement.

God causes the sun to rise on both the bad and the good. Likewise he sends the rain to both the just and the unjust. Just look around you! God is generous to both the ungrateful and the wicked.

Mark 12:28-37; Matthew 22:34-40; Luke 10:25-28

Jesus answers a question as to which commandment is most important: Hear O Israel, the LORD our God is one LORD. And you shall love the LORD your God with all of your heart, and with all of your soul, with all of your mind, and all of your strength. And the second greatest commandment is this: You shall love your neighbor as yourself. There are no commandments in the entire Old Testament more important than these two. If you keep these, you will keep all of the others automatically.

Consider this: A certain man was traveling from Jerusalem to Jericho. Unfortunately for him, robbers were hiding in the hills and they attacked him, took his belongings, and beat him nearly to death. They left his bruised and bloody body by the roadside. About 30 minutes after the robbery, a Priest came down the road. When he saw the man, he went way around him so that the man would not make him ritually "unclean." A little while later a temple assistant was coming down the road. He too saw the man, but didn't want to get involved. Finally a man from Samaria, a despised "half-breed" Jew, was coming down the road. When he saw the poor beaten man he was moved with compassion. He ran to him and bandaged his wounds and treated them with medicine. Then he put the man on his own donkey and walked beside him all the way into town. He took him to a motel and paid the man's bill. He left some extra money at the front office, just in case the man needed it to get back on his feet. Now I ask you: Which of these three men in the story was a "neighbor" to the injured man?

Mark 2:23-28; Matthew 12:1-8; Luke 6:1-5

The Sabbath day was created *for* Humans; Not humans for the Sabbath day. The Sabbath day of worship was ordained to enlighten Mankind, not to be a senseless burden. However, the Son of Man is Lord even over the Sabbath.

Matthew 22:2-13; Luke 14:15-24

A man was planning a big party and invited many guests. At 4:30pm, he sent his butler to tell the guests that the feast was ready. But one by one they made lame excuses why they couldn't come. Angered by the lack of appreciation, the man told his butler to go out in the streets and invite everyone. But even then, there were still seats available at the table. Then the man said: "Invite everyone in the world; anyone who can walk or drag themselves to the party. I insist that my house be filled!"

John 8:3-11

To the woman caught in the act of adultery: You are free to go, but, sin no more.

Luke 15:11-32

Once there was a man with two teenage sons. The younger of the two came to his father and said, "Father. I am nearly an adult and ready to leave home and start my own life. Please give me my inheritance in advance." The father agreed and went ahead and divided a large amount of money between the two boys.

Not long after that, the younger son packed his things and left for the big city to find himself. But when he arrived he soon got in with the wrong crowd and behaved recklessly. Within 6 months he had spent his entire inheritance and had nothing to show for it. Unfortunately for him, just when he was approaching "rock bottom," the economy hit a terrible slump and there were no jobs available. In some places people couldn't even get enough to eat. He began to actually fear for his life and was overwhelmed with guilt. He finally managed to get a menial job as a pig-herder on the outskirts of the city. He became so hungry that he would sometimes steal some of the slop from the pigs and eat it himself.

Then one day, he came to his senses. He realized that even the servants that worked at his father's mansion had it better than he did! So he formulated a plan: "I will go to my father on my knees, and beg for his forgiveness. I will then pledge myself to him for life, as one of his servants." So the man stopped what he was doing and began the long journey back to his father's property.

While he was still far off in the distance his father saw him coming. His heart melted at the sight of his lost son and he ran out to meet him. He threw his arms around his son and kissed him with joy. And with that, the prodigal son said, "Father, I have sinned against God and against you. I no longer deserve to be called your son. Please consider me as one of your servants."

However, the Father commanded his slaves, "Quickly! Get my finest coat and put it around his shoulders! Bring him my favorite gold ring from the top of my dresser! Tell the cooks to prepare our yearly feast early – today! We have something much more important to celebrate than the harvest! This son of mine was dead; but has come back to life. He was lost, but now he is found!" And everyone began to celebrate.

Now the older son, the one who had stayed and had been working daily for the Father, was out in the field working while all of this was going on. As he dragged his tired body home he heard music and dancing at the main house. He asked a servant boy what was going on.

The boy told him, "Your long lost brother is back! He has changed his ways and his heart! And, your father has thrown a great party to celebrate his return."

The older son grew angry and reused to go to the party. His father saw him outside pouting and went out to talk with him. He said to his father, "All these years I have slaved for you. I have been a good son. I have not wasted your money or disobeyed your orders. However, you have never once thrown a party for me. But when my deadbeat brother shows up you throw this feast!?"

To this the father replied, "My son; you have always been at my side. Everything that I have has been yours. But we *had* to celebrate! Your brother was *dead*, but he has come back to life. He was lost, but is now found."

Matthew 7:9-11; Luke 11:11-13

Would anyone among you hand your child a stone when he asked for bread? Would you hand him a snake if he was asking for a fish? Of course you wouldn't! If mere mortals, as unscrupulous as they are, still know how to give appropriate gifts to their children, isn't it even more likely that the Father in Heaven will give good things to those who ask of him?

Mark 3:20-21;31-35; Matthew 12:46-50; Luke 8:19-21; John 10:20

"Who are my mother and brothers?" And looking around the crowd of disciples in the house, making eye contact with each of them, he added, "Right here are my mother and brothers. Whoever thirsts for the Will of God – he or she is my brother, sister, or mother!"

Mark 3:1-5; Matthew 12:9-13; Luke 6:6-10

Is it permissible to do good or evil on the Sabbath day? Is it better on the Sabbath day to save life or to destroy it?

Mark 10:31; Matthew 20:1-15

The last will be first and the first shall be last.

The Kingdom of Heaven is like a boss who went out at 7:00 A.M. to hire laborers for his farm. He agreed to pay them $50 for the days work, and sent them into the fields. At about 9:00 A.M. he went into town to visit the store and saw some young men bumming around outside. He told them that he had work for them and that he would pay them a fair wage to work his fields. They agreed and went back to the farm with him. He continued this process of going into town looking for laborers all day. Many men were hired. The last group joined the crew after 5:00 P.M. At 6:00 P.M., the whistle blew, and the men lined up to be paid. Everyone who worked that day received $50, one at a time. The men who worked all day were astonished! "Why did you pay those guys who worked only an hour the same amount that you paid us?" The boss replied, "I agreed to pay you $50, did I not? Did I wrong you? Isn't it my prerogative to pay my workers any wage I want? Your problem is that you are envious and jealous, when I am only trying to show generosity!"

Mark 1:29-42; 2:1-12; Luke 4:38-44

My child, your sins are forgiven.

Mark 7:24-30; Matthew 15:21-28

Because of your persistence and faith your daughter is healed. When you get home you will find her well.

Mark 14:43-15:37; Luke 22:52-53; John 18:2-12;
I Corinthians 15:8

Do you not know that all those who live by the sword, die by the sword?

Human Nature(s)

The normative nature of humankind contrasted with the nature of God. It also includes the idea of the two natures of man: The carnal self contrasted with the spiritual self.

Luke 16:1-8

There once was a business owner whose Chief Executive Officer had been accused of squandering the owner's capital. The business' owner called him into his office and said, What is this I have heard about your behavior? I am ordering an audit of your files effective immediately. If things aren't on the up-and-up, you will be most certainly terminated!" The C.E.O. was terrified. He thought to himself, "What am I going to do? I have invested my life into this career. I am too proud to go on welfare." So he began to formulate a plan. The C.E.O. called in each of the business owner's debtors. He said to the first, "How much do you owe the company?" The man replied, "Five thousand dollars." The C.E.O. said to him, "Here is yourinvoice – let's just make it $2,500 and call it even." Then the C.E.O. called in another debtor who owed ten thousand dollars to the company. "If you give me $8,000 today, I'll tear up your invoice." When word got back to the owner, he actually *praised* the dishonest C.E.O. for his shrewdness; for the children of this world in their time and place are wiser than the children of light.

Mark 10:13-15; Matthew 18:3, 19:13-15; Luke 18:15-17

Let the children come to me. Do not get in their way. You must realize that the Kingdom of God belongs to people just like that. In fact, if a person cannot accept God like a child does, they cannot really accept God at all.

Mark 2:18-22; Matthew 9:14-15; Luke 5:33-34

People don't like to change their old customs and habits. Nobody wants to switch from their favorite food or drink that they have eaten all their life and try something new on a mere whim. People feel the same way about new ideas as they do new foods. They don't like change – sometimes to their great detriment.

Mark 6:1-6; Matthew 13:54-58

No prophet goes without respect except in his home country and among his relatives.

Mark 1:12-13; Matthew 4:1-11; Luke 4:1-13

Human beings are not to live on bread alone, but on every word that comes from the mouth of God.

Matthew 11:16-19; Luke 7:31-35

What is this world like? What is it *really* like? The people of this world are like little children at the park playing together and singing a song: *We played the flute for you, but you wouldn't dance; then we sang a sad song, but you wouldn't cry.*

My cousin John appeared in this world refusing fine foods and wine and you said he was "too extreme." But the Son of Man has not observed any particular dietary regimen and eats the same foods as his disciples and you say that he is a 'loose-liver' and a friend to scumbags and criminals. But I tell you, Wisdom is justified by her children.

Luke 18:2-5

Once there was a powerful judge. He lived in a small town where he was familiar to the townspeople. He prided himself on being a "self-made man." He wasn't particularly religious, and had no patience for people who wasted his time. In the same town, there was a widow who came to his office just about every week and demanded: "Please consider my case against this person I am suing!"

For a long time the judge resisted. The case just didn't seem important enough to warrant his attention. However, the widow's persistence at last wore him down. He said to himself, " I am afraid of nothing, and no one. However, I am going to help this woman just so that she will go away and stop pestering me!" Such is the way of this world. Even though the judge has no genuine compassion for the woman, he eventually helped her because of her persistence.

Mark 12:1-8; 14:1-7; Luke 7:36-39

A person owned a vineyard and rented it to some farmers so that they collect the crop for him. After a while he sent one of his slaves to the vineyard to collect the profits. But the farmers grabbed the slave, beat him almost to death and sent him back to the owner of the vineyard. The owner thought to himself, "Perhaps these men made a mistake. Maybe they didn't realize that it was *my* slave." So he sent another slave with an official seal. However, the farmers beat this slave as well. So the owner said to himself, "I will send my son. Surely they will show respect for him." But when the owner's son showed up at the vineyard, they grabbed him and beat him to death; knowing he was the rightful heir to the vineyard.

Mark 10:35-45; Luke 22:24-27; John 10:34; Psalm 82

As you well know, those who rule this world do it with an iron hand. They believe that giving orders and having lots of followers are the measure of leadership. But they are wrong. If you want to be truly great then focus on serving others, not on giving orders. The greatest of all will be the one who is the servant of all. Let me be clear. I was not born so that I could be waited on hand-and-foot. Nor have I aspired to lead by force. If fact, before long, I will give my very life as a martyr: an example for many to follow. The spark of the divine rests in us all.

Remember the psalm Asaph sang for the Lord (Psalm 82): *They know not, neither will they understand. They walk on in darkness, as the foundation of the Earth is out of course. I have said, "You all are gods, and children of the Sovereign Lord." But you all will die as mere men, the workers as well as the princes. Arise, O God. Judge this earth! Thy Kingdom come!*

Mark 14:43-15:37; Luke 22:52-53; John 18:2-12

Do you not know that all those who live by the sword, die by the sword?

Mark 12:1-8; 14:1-7; Luke 7:36-39

You will always have the poor with you and you can do good to them whenever you feel like it. However, I will not be here much longer.

Matthew 18:12-13; Luke 15:4-9

If a woman has ten silver coins and misplaces only one of them, won't she keep searching until she finds it? In fact, she will frantically look in every corner of the house with her flashlight until the coin is found. Then the woman will call her friends to let them know the good news! "Celebrate with me," she will say, "the coin I lost has been found!"

If a shepherd owns a hundred sheep and only one of them wonders off, what will he do? He will leave the ninety-nine at home and go looking for the little lost sheep. When he finds it, he we lift it up on him shoulders and smile. And, like the woman with he lost coin, he will call his friends to help him celebrate his discovery!

Compassion

The desire and habit of alleviating the pain of another person.

Mark 1:29-42; 2:1-12; Luke 4:38-44

When Jesus saw their simple faith and trust, he said (looking at the paralyzed man), "My child, your sins are forgiven." Some in the audience wondered to themselves, "Why does he say such things? Doesn't he know that only God can forgive sins?" Jesus sensed their doubts and addressed them: "Why are you entertaining such questions? Is it easier to say 'your sins are forgiven,' or 'pick up your mat and walk'?"

Then, the man got up, picked up his mat, and walked out as everyone looked on. Most of the crowd became ecstatic and spontaneously erupted in praise to God. One proclaimed, "We have never seen anything like this before!"

John 5:2-9

Jesus approached him and asked, "Do you want to get well?" The man replied, "Sir, I don't have anyone to put me in the pool when the water is agitated. Every time I try to make my way someone beats me to it." Moved with compassion Jesus responded, "Get up, pick up your mat and walk." The man recovered at once and picked up his mat as Jesus said.

Non-attachment

The notion that attachment to the material world is a source of dissatisfaction and spiritual alienation from God.

Matthew 6:25-30; Luke 12:22-31

Don't spend your energy worrying about life – what you are going to eat, or about clothing for your body. There is so much more to living than food and clothing. Think about the birds: they don't plant or harvest, they don't have storehouses or barns. Yet God feeds them. Don't you realize that you are worth so much more than birds? God even knows the number of the hairs upon your head.

Can you add even one hour to your life by fretting about it? So if you can't even do that, why worry about anything? Think of the wildflowers: they neither worry nor sweat. Yet, even Solomon was never dressed as fine as them. If God so takes care of the plants in the field which are here today and gone tomorrow, is it not surely more likely that he has your best welfare in mind? Don't take anything for granted!

Matthew 8:19-22; Luke 9:57-58

Let the dead bury their own dead; but *you* come and join me in announcing the Kingdom of God.

Foxes have dens, and birds have nests; but the Son of Man has nowhere to rest his head.

Matthew 5:39-41; Luke 6:29-30

The best way to deal with violence is to not react violently to an evil person. In fact, if someone should slap you on the right cheek, give them your left as well. When you react to violence you get drawn into the violence and risk doing evil as well.

If someone threatens to sue you for your coat, give them your coat and your shirt as well. And, even if the Roman officers force you to carry their goods an entire mile, then walk a second mile as well – all without anger. Do not feed the energy of a violent and evil person.

You must struggle to get in through the narrow door. Many will try to get in, but few will persevere. And I will tell you an even more difficult saying along these lines. Unless a person completely dedicates himself to the quest for God, that is, puts God ahead of all other relationships; mother, brother, sisters, he cannot be my true disciple.

Mark 6:14-29; Matthew 14:1-12

When you went out to the wilderness to see John preach, what did you go to see? Grass blowing in the wind? What did you really go out to see? A man dressed in an expensive suit? But wait! Those who wear fine clothes are found in fancy buildings with a corner office.

Matthew 5:39-41; Luke 6:29-30

In your dealings with the world be as sly as snakes but as innocent as doves.

5

The Story in
Catechismal Format

The following is a learning guide written in the traditional style of the Christian catechism, but based on the teachings of the Historical Jesus. The Westminster Catechism was used as a rough model for the basic format for the following catechism because of its widespread use, availability, and historical significance.

Q. 1. What is the chief and highest end of human beings?

A. The chief and highest end of human beings is to grow in God, and to fully enjoy him forever.

Q. 2. How does one know that God exists?

A. By evidence that can be found within oneself as well as the physical evidence of the inhabited world.

Q. 3. How does God speak to us?

A. God speaks all the time. We need but to listen. God is revealed in our hearts and experiences – especially in the small still places. Scripture is a record of the history of the evolution in understanding of God over time. Jesus was and is the culmination of this process.

Q. 4. What did Jesus principally teach?

A. Seek out and Love the Lord your God with all your heart, mind, and soul. And, love your neighbor every bit as much as you love yourself.

Q. 5. Where is God?

A. God is everywhere at all times.

Q. 6. What is the chief characteristic of God?

A. God is Love. God forgives all. God is generous to both the ungrateful and the wicked.

Q. 7. Who is God?

A. God is beyond our comprehension and cannot be defined except in metaphor. God is everything there is. God is Love. God is Wisdom. God is the Word.

Q. 8. What is the work of creation?

A. God made all there is; is all there is, and what God made is good.

Q. 9. What is unique about humankind?

A. Human beings are unique among God's creation in that they have the power to choose, to be responsible for their choices, and to guide their own development.

Q. 10. What are God's works of providence?

A. All things work together for good; for our learning, growth and spiritual development.

Q. 11. Why is there so much sin and suffering in the world?

A. Suffering is caused by neglecting one's pursuit of God, being wrapped up in the carnal self and by ignoring the needs of others.

Q. 12. What is the Carnal Self?

A. The Carnal Self is the animal part of us. It is the pleasure-seeking and self-seeking dimension of the human animal. The Carnal Self is part of God's creation and is thus "good." However, it is not the "real" us.

Q. 13. What is the Spiritual Self?

A. The Spiritual Self is the only real self. It is the seat of our real conscience and our closest connection to God. The Spiritual Self never dies.

Q. 14. Who can be saved?

A. Salvation is a process that begins with the realization that one is responsible for one's actions and that one is essentially spiritual in nature. Anyone can take the path to salvation.

Q. 15. Why would anyone want to be "saved?"

A. Growth and advancement are the natural course of all things. The further one moves along the path, the higher capacity one has for understanding. This includes the understanding of pleasure and pain and their proper place.

Q. 16. What is Sanctification?

A. Sanctification is the gradual process of growing towards God. As we approach God we manifest more of his characteristics.

Q. 17. Can a person feel assured that they will be with God some day, no matter what has transpired?

A. All things work together for good for those who love the Lord. God does not desire that even one of his little ones should parish.

Q. 18. What does it mean to be "in communion?"

A. Jesus demonstrated and taught that we could show our

love for God by loving others. Everyone is connected and interdependent at a deep spiritual level.

Q. 19. What is "Death?"
A. There is no death. "Death" is our word for a change that occurs at the end of every person's physical life.

Q. 20. Should we worry about death?
A. It is not helpful to worry about anything. God has our best welfare in mind. The final outcome is assured to be in our best interest.

Q. 21. What is the duty which God requires of man?
A. To seek him above all else and with every part of our being; our minds, our souls, our emotions, and our actions.

Q. 22. What Does Jesus say about considering the sins of others?
A. That the standard we use to judge them will be the standard by which we are judged. We ought then, to focus on our own journey of faith and leave others to their own.

Q. 23. How did Jesus demonstrate love?
A. By acting with compassion at all times.

Q. 24. Where is the Kingdom of God?
A. The Kingdom of God is within us, without us, and everywhere.

Q. 25. In what sense is Jesus the "Word of God?"
A. Jesus is the personification and incarnation of God's wisdom and power.

Q. 26. What is the sacrament of communion?
A. The sacrament of communion is an earthly symbol and ritual of the spiritual truth that all people are one, and that God and human beings are one.

Q. 27. What is prayer?
A. Prayer is being spiritually connected to God and to his will.

Q. 28. What is the "Lord's Prayer?"

A. The Lord's Prayer is the only recorded prayer specifically recommended to us by Jesus.

Q. 29. What are the elements of the Lord's Prayer?

A. The elements of the Lord's Prayer are chiefly four: 1) A petition to and celebration of our connectedness to God; 2) a petition for basic physical needs; 3) a celebration and thankfulness for God's Kingdom, and; 4) a petition for the power to forgive others.

Afterword

I have reserved this, the final portion of the book, to divulge my personal reflections on the man, Jesus. Although I believe in good conscience that my opinions follow from the evidence, they are nevertheless my personal opinions and should be considered as separate from the more rigorous and factual approach of the earlier chapters of this book. Since I have already made it clear that this section is set aside for my personal reflections, I have dispensed with repeating "in my opinion," as well as avoidance of personal pronouns.

Who was Jesus? In the briefest possible terms, Jesus was a high consciousness mystic – perhaps the highest level mystic that has yet been born. A "mystic" is a person who cultivates a direct experience of the transcendent – and in Jesus' case, shares the insights with others. I believe this is, in fact, what Jesus meant by "prayer." Clearly, Jesus was also a man of great compassion-in-action; however, this compassion was a natural by-product of his close relationship with God rather than an end in itself.

Jesus had much in common with other Eastern mystics both in message and behavior. His essential message was to grow close to God (i.e. "The Kingdom of God"), and in so doing, take responsibility for one's spiritual evolution. One's progress along this path could be measured, according to Jesus, by the capacity one has to **love** one's fellow human being.

Although it is certainly not explicit in his words, I suspect that Yeshua Barnasha believed in some sort of reincarnation as well. Practically every high-level mystic, regardless of background or religion, has professed belief in some type of reincarnation. This includes many Western Christian mystics. Thus, I further suspect that Jesus saw this spiritual growth as a process that might take many lifetimes.

Obviously this Jesus differs greatly from the commonly-held (especially fundamentalist) conceptions of Jesus. However, I do not believe that Jesus ever claimed to be a "sacrifice for sin" (Atonement) in any juridical, literal sense of the terms. As discussed in the Foreword, this Atonement Theology is largely absent in the synoptic gospels (Matthew, Mark, and Luke). The Jesus of the book of Mark, even before being subject to critical analysis and alteration, is strikingly similar to the words and message of other mystical sages. Jesus' message of Karma, Relationship-with-God, Compassion-Towards-Others, and the dichotomy of the Spiritual Man vs. the Carnal Man is almost indistinguishable from the core message of Buddha and Krishna.

So, is there any "Good News" here? The Good News is you can't loose. Every honest and sincere "good thing" you have ever done has had a positive impact on your development. That is the Law. There is more good news. God is not "up in the sky." He is as close as your heart. The fastest and most reliable way to find God is to look within.

Although the game is "rigged" to facilitate your (and everyone else's) spiritual development, it is possible to accelerate one's path to enlightenment and growth in consciousness. According to Jesus this is done by (in order of Jesus' emphasis); 1) Consciously deciding to put the quest for God first in one's life, 2) Consistently living from one's Spirit instead of carnal desires, 3) By practicing (literally) compassion towards others, and 4) not-attachment to physical things.

Notes

Chapter 1: Prologue to a True Story

[1]I submit this "creed" as a proposed amalgamation of the creedal statements common to many large mainstream Christian denominations. The Southern Baptist Convention is one such example. Harold Bloom also has a nice treatment of the topic in his book, The American Religion (1992), in which he defines the core of American Christianity in five dimensions: 1) The Bible is always right; 2) Jesus was born of a virgin; 3) Jesus' suffering substitutes for our sin; 4) Jesus rose from the dead, and 5) Jesus will return again. (cf pp. 224).

[2]This addition shows up most clearly in denominations/groups most influenced by Calvinism, which include some Baptists, Presbyterians, Reformed, as well as many "independent" Christian groups.

[3]This is the general scholarly consensus. (cf The Oxford Annotated Bible NRSV, Interpreter's Bible, N.I.V. Study Bible, and many others).

[4]The earliest known Christian creed is expounded by Paul in I Corinthians, chapter 15. Most scholars assume that he is repeating a known liturgical or creedal formula in I Corinthians 15:3-6. This creed was recorded at least ten years before the book of Mark was written and contains no references to the Atonement. However, Paul adds it in the expansion that follows in Chapter 15. The Atonement is a centerpiece of Pauline theology. The Gospel of John may also reflect Paul's influence.

[5]Some may balk at the apparent hubris of this statement. True, it is difficult to quantify and thus measure. However, I think circumstantial qualification is fairly ubiquitous. For example, on the Internet, over 34.8 million entries were found for "Jesus Sacrifice." Compare this to 16.8 million entries for "Love Your Enemies."

[6]cf The Five Gospels, by Funk (1996); The Son of Man Debate, by Burkett (1999); The Historical Jesus in Recent Research by Dunn, et al. (2005).

[7]See the Topical section of this book for an expanded definition of Karma.

Chapter 2: Introduction to Jesus

[1]See note #6

[2]Catechism is the traditional name for an officially sanctioned Christian learning guide.

[3]I am not necessarily making the case that Paul invented Atonement Theology on his own – only that he believed it and popularized it.

[4]The general consensus is that extra-biblical sources have added very little to the overall accuracy of the Gospel accounts. In this paper, they account for less than 2% of the overall reconstructed text. According to The Jesus Seminar, the most important of the extra-biblical sources are The Gospel of Thomas, Oxyrhynchus 1224, The Egerton Gospel, and a few passages from Eusebius' Ecclesiastical History.

[5]cf Mark 4:1-20; Mark 12:30-31; Matthew 6:24-34; Luke 17:21; John 13:34

Chapter 3: The Story in Chronological Order

[1]Probably an early liturgical poem affixed to the Gospel of John. Note the poem does not specifically identify Jesus as "The Word." The "Word" has a long

history in the Jewish tradition as the emissary of the wisdom, purpose, and energy of God.

[2]The reader will obviously notice the lack of birth narratives. In the oldest accounts, they do not exist, nor are they referred to. The surviving accounts show inconsistencies and are difficult to harmonize.

[3]Many scholars have speculated that Jesus was originally a follower of John. This is not specific in the narrative, but it does seem like a reasonable speculation that fits the available facts.

[4]In Aramaic, the 22nd Psalm begins "Eloi Eloi Lama Sabachthani."

[5]The oldest sources do not contain clear resurrection narratives. The earliest documentable source of information is the words of Paul and he seems to interpret Jesus' resurrection in a spiritual rather than a literally physical sense. His words on the subject were composed before any of the gospels. See I Corinthians 15, particularly vs. 5-8. Also see John 20:14-17

[6]*cf* Matthew 26:32; 28:7

Bibliography/Sources

American Standard Version of the Holy Bible (1901). Public domain.

Armstrong, K.A. (1993). A History of God: The 4,000-Year Quest of Judaism, Christianity, and Islam. Ballantine Books, New York.

Bercot, David W. (2003). The Kingdom that Turned the World Upside Down. Scroll Publishing, Amberson, PA.

Bloom, Harold (1992). The American Religion. Simon & Schuster, New York.

The Book of Common Prayer (1928). Oxford University Press, New York, NY.

Book of Confessions: Study Edition (1996). Geneva Press, Louisville, KY.

Borg, M. (2004). Jesus and Buddha: The Parallel Sayings. Ulysses Press, Berkeley, CA.

Borg, M. (1995). Meeting Jesus Again for the First Time: The Historical Jesus and the Heart of Contemporary Faith. Harper One, New York.

Burkett, Delbert (1999). The Son of Man Debate: A History and Evaluation. Cambridge University Press. New York.

Carse, J.P. (1997). The Gospel of the Beloved Disciple. Harper, San Francisco.

The Complete Bible: An American Translation (1951). Edgar J. Goodspeed (Ed.). The University of Chicago Press.

Crossan, John D. (1992). The Historical Jesus: The Life of a Mediterranean Jewish Peasant. Harper, San Francisco.

Danizier, Davis D. (1998). Betrayal of Jesus: Twenty-First Century Challenges for Christians. Word Wizards Publications, Escondido, CA.

Ehrman, B.D. (2007). Misquoting Jesus: The Story Behind Who Changed the Bible and Why. Harper One, New York.

Funk, Robert W. (1999). The Gospel of Jesus: According to the Jesus Seminar. Polebridge Press, Santa Rosa, CA.

Girzone, Joseph F. (2000). Jesus, His Life and Teachings. Image Books, New York, NY.

Goodspeed, E.J. (1956). A Life of Jesus. Harper Torchlight, New York.

Interpreters Bible (1951). Nolan B. Harmon (Ed.). Abingdon Press, New York.

The King James Bible (1611). Public domain in the United States of America.

Keating, Thomas (2006). Open Mind, Open Heart: 20th Anniversary Edition. Continuum Books, New York.

Kinnaman, D., & Lyons, G. (2007). Un-Christian: What a New Generation Really Thinks About Christianity and Why it Matters. Baker Books, Grand Rapids, MI.

Jefferson, Thomas (1820). The Life and Morals of Jesus of Nazareth. [various publishers].

Marion, Jim (2004). Death of the Mythic God: The Rise of Evolutionary Spirituality. Hampton Roads Publishing, Charlottesville, VA.

Marion, Jim (2000). Putting on the Mind of Christ. Hampton Roads Publishing, Charlottesville, VA.

McKenzie, J.L. (1965). Dictionary of the Bible. Macmillan, New York.

McLaren, B.D. (2006). A Generous Orthodoxy. Zondervan, Grand Rapids, MI.

Meyer, Marvin (2005). The Unknown Sayings of Jesus. New Seeds Publishing, Boston.

Myers, D.G. (1992). The Pursuit of Happiness: Discovering the Pathway to Fulfillment, Well-Being, and Enduring Personal Joy. Quill Publishing, New York, NY.

New Analytical Bible and Dictionary of the Bible. (1973). Dickson, J.A. (Ed.). World Bible Publishers, Iowa Falls, IA.

NIV Study Bible. (2002). Barker, K.L. & Burdick (Eds.). Zondervan, Grand Rapids, MI.

The Oxford Dictionary of the Christian Church, Third Edition. (2005). Cross, F.L., & Livingstone, E.A. (Eds.). Oxford University Press, USA.

Packer, J.I., Merrill, C.T., & White, W.W. (1982). The World of the New Testament. Thomas Nelson, Nashville.

Reimarus, Herman Samuel (1768). Fragments. [various publishers].

Sanders, E.P. (1977). Paul and Palestinian Judaism: A Comparison of Patterns of Religion. Fortress Press, Philadelphia.

Shanks, Hershel (1993). An Unpublished Dead Sea Scroll Text Parallels Luke's Infancy Narrative. In H. Shanks (Ed.), Understanding the Dead Sea Scrolls (pp. 203-204). New York: Vintage Books.

Synopsis of the Four Gospels (1993). Kurt Aland (Ed.). German Bible Society, Stuttgart.

Tolle, E. (2004). The Power of Now: A Guide to Spiritual Enlightenment. New World Library, Novato, CA.

Vanderkam, James C. (1993). The Dead Sea Scrolls and Christianity. In H. Shanks (Ed.), Understanding the Dead Sea Scrolls (pp. 181-202). New York: Vintage Books.

Vermes, Geza (1983). Jesus and the World of Judaism. Fortress Press. Minneapolis.

Vivekananda (1902). Karma Yoga: The Yoga of Action. Trio Process Printers, Kolkata, India.

Vivekananda (1982). Raja-Yoga, Paperback Edition. Ramakrishna-Vivekananda Center Books, New York.

Wilson, Ian (1984). Jesus: The Evidence. Harper, San Francisco, CA.

Wright, N.T. (1999). The Challenge of Jesus: Rediscovering Who Jesus Was and Is. IVP Academic Press, Downers Grove, Il.

Yadin, Yigael (1993). The Temple Scroll. In H. Shanks (Ed.), <u>Understanding the Dead Sea Scrolls</u> (pp. 87-112). New York: Vintage Books.

Yogananda, P. (2007). <u>The Yoga of Jesus.</u> Self-Realization Fellowship Publishing, Los Angeles.

Zukav, Gary (1999). <u>The Seat of the Soul.</u> Simon and Schuster, New York, NY.

www.ingramcontent.com/pod-product-compliance
Lightning Source LLC
Chambersburg PA
CBHW062018040426
42447CB00010B/2047